About the Author

Since 1999 **VALERIE MENARD** has been a freelance writer and editor based in Austin, Texas. She is a former editor for *Hispanic* magazine and advice columnist for *Moderna*. She is a contributing editor to *Latina Style* and regular advice columnist for *Hispanic Online*. The author of *The Latino Holiday Book* and a second-generation Latina, Menard is an advocate for Latino arts and culture.

Valerie Menard

Latinas
in
Love

A Modern Guide to

Love and Relationships

MARLOWE & COMPANY
NEW YORK

Library of Congress Control Number: 2002113882

ISBN 1-56924-512-6

9 8 7 6 5 4 3 2

Designed by Pauline Neuwirth, Neuwirth & Associates, Inc.

Printed in the United States of America

To my husband Reid

Contents

Preface

"All you need is love"

$\mathcal{M}$ANY HAVE TRIED to capture the emotions associated with love in words and song, but I think the Beatles said it best. I've always been fascinated by people, relationships, and romance. There really is nothing so sweet as true love or so bitter as unrequited love. The ways in which men and women wander through this romantic labyrinth amaze and intrigue me. I love to dissect relationships and predict their success or failure by psychoanalyzing behavior and motivation. And I have always been free with advice for my friends, though initially I was a bit of a despot about it. Eventually I realized that people—especially women—will always do exactly what they want, and at best, advice will only plant a seed of truth that will hopefully germinate sometime down the road.

I admit, I found it frustrating to give advice that was repeatedly ignored. "If you're not going to listen to my advice, then you might as well talk to a wall," I scolded one friend. My attitude softened after I noticed a pattern. The female friends who tended to listen the least had the lowest self-esteem, whereas boys almost always took my advice. My task became to pump up the girls' egos rather than tell them what to do, but even the best confidence coach will find her efforts futile if her client has no faith in herself.

I was blessed with a clear knowledge of who I am and what I want, both in life and in love. It's partly due to my astrological sign; Aquarians are *über* individuals, but mostly it's a gift from my mom, who definitely taught me to respect and value myself. Moms like mine, however, are not as common as I had believed. Without that kind of early positive reinforcement, it's very hard to be confident as an adult. These women never developed the ability to figure out what was best for them. All my coaching was useless because they didn't feel worthy of receiving love and respect.

When it came time to decide what I wanted to do when I grew up, surprisingly, I chose to study journalism and English in college, although I did take one psychology course. Writing was my vocation, giving advice my avocation. But when the opportunity came ten years after I graduated to write an advice column for Latinas, it was kismet.

In 1996, *Hispanic* magazine spun off a new publication targeting Latinas called *Moderna*. I remember the editorial planning sessions we held—I was an editor for *Hispanic*, and the staff members were asked to do double duty on *Moderna*—with the magazine's editor, Christine Granados, and the publisher, Alfredo Estrada. They asked us to come up with ideas for features and departments that would run regularly in the magazine. I not only suggested that we run a regular advice column, I jumped at the chance to write it, and we called it "Preguntas para Pilar." Initially, letters were solicited from friends and staff, but as soon as the first official letter came in, I was thrilled. I've always felt strongly about promoting girl power and this was my chance to get other women excited about who they are and encourage them to feel good about themselves. This was my chance to do for them what I had tried to do for my friends so long ago.

Moderna survived for three years. In 1999, *Hispanic* moved from Austin to Miami and I began my odyssey as a freelance writer. It wasn't long before *Hispanic* launched its revamped Web site, Hispanic Online, and I was back in business with an advice column, this time as Amiga Mía. I'm still offering advice online to this day, and the problems are still very much the same, though some have a technological slant. Over the years I have accumulated a lot of correspondence and each chapter in this book begins with a composite letter addressed either to Pilar or Amiga Mía.

As a freelancer, I've had many wonderful opportunities, but one of the greatest was the chance to write my first book, *The Latino Holiday Book*. That project was the brainchild of my agent, Laura Dail. This book is mine. I wanted a chance to expand my mission to a broader group of Latinas and help them learn to love themselves. This is not a clinical or empirical study. These are my thoughts about relationships based on my experience as an advice columnist, a friend, and a Latina. I did, however, solicit the thoughts and opinions of Latinas as well as non-Latinas for the book. To do this, I put together a Latinas in Love survey (which you can view in its entirety in the Appendix) that was distributed to women via email. The response rate was 20 percent, 67 percent of whom were Latinas. The majority of the respondents were between the ages of thirty-two and forty-five. Ninety-three percent of the respondents were college educated and 99 percent were employed. Responses to the survey are included throughout the book.

Latinas in Love focuses on heterosexual relationships, but that's not to say that there isn't a large contingent of lesbian Latinas who have relationship issues as well. My decision not to refer to it is merely a reflection of my lack of expertise on the subject, not a denial of its existence or validity. I think the topic deserves a whole book, not just a token chapter.

Based on the results of my survey, I found that for Latinas, the basic ingredients for a good relationship are consistent with those of any woman. Latinas want love, respect, admiration, and desire from a potential mate. What makes Latinas unique, however, is the cultural lessons we've learned and tap into when we become involved in a romance. In many cases, those tools have become outdated and, in some cases, even destructive. Modern Latinas know that they will lead very different lives than their mothers, and one of the biggest issues they struggle with is the ever-widening gap between their modern American life and the expectations of their often deeply traditional families.

To date, there hasn't been a self-help book devoted to Latinas and relationships. Our biggest challenge is to sustain our self-confidence, but with the ongoing identity crisis facing Latinas today, I felt it was important to write a book that reminds us that being a woman is definitely a good thing, but being a Latina is truly grand. We need to stop doubting ourselves and start trusting our instincts. We need to realize that we can be modern *and* traditional. We never have to choose between our roots and our modern American lives, no matter how strongly we're pressured to pick a side. This is who we are and understanding and accepting that is the first step toward figuring out what we want out of life and love.

I hope this book gives Latinas a clearer and more positive perspective on who they are and what they want. Hopefully, a Latina who reads this book will find the tools for building her confidence so that she can more easily decide what she wants in life and love, whether or not that includes a husband. Through self-discovery and self-respect, true love is found.

Sinceramente,
Valerie Menard

1

Thoroughly Modern Maria

Who is the new Latina and what kind of relationship does she want?

Dear Pilar,

I'm very proud to be a Latina. I still feel self-conscious about it, but I know that generations ago it was even more difficult to be a Latina in the U.S. As I get older and meet other women in the workplace, I'm torn between what I've been taught and what I see. I don't want to lose my culture, but when it comes to relationships, a lot of what's expected of women in our culture seems really outdated. I want to be treated as an equal and a goddess. Is that too much to ask?

Julia, 23

RECEIVED THIS LETTER and many like it in my position as an advice columnist for *Moderna* magazine and Hispanic Online. I have heard this question voiced many times, and I understand completely where it is coming from. I don't know about you, but as a Latina, I get the feeling that it's great to be me! I don't simply just feel happy to be in my shoes, I want to be loud and proud about it. However, I still get that nagging feeling, from time to time, that God might punish me if I am.

Perhaps my celebratory mood is due to the fact that finally the modern Latina is in vogue. The standards of beauty in America today now include Latinas' features, figures, and flair. Fashion, whether created at the hands of Latino style icons like Oscar de la Renta and Carolina Herrera or non-Latino designers like Valentino, reflects a "Latina-ness" that is colorful, feminine, and sexy. From the silver screen to MTV, Latinas have become more visible and more in demand. Whether in a suit, a purse, or in a person's skin tone, brown is suddenly beautiful.

Perhaps it began with the "Latin explosion" in music in the late 1990s, but little by little, high-profile Latinas are emerging in the entertainment industry. They aren't just one-hit-wonders or one-movie-wonders—they've endured. Today, young ambassadresses for the modern Latina, such as Jennifer Lopez, Christina Aguilera, and Shakira, command media attention and achieve great success. As modern Latinas, they're beautiful, but they're also ambitious and extremely motivated. They not only have the talent to succeed, they are willing to match that talent with effort. Christina, Shakira, and Jennifer reveal the real truth about modern Latinas—they're as tough and hardworking as they are sexy. Add to these characteristics the main features of a modern woman—independence, education, and career-mindedness—and like Jennifer, Christina, and Shakira, all modern Latinas are poised for superstardom!

¡Pues, ojalá!

In reality, the modern Latina certainly has the potential to be all this and more, but she is at a crossroads. She's poised for greatness, but she's still shackled by issues related to tradition, language, and prejudice. She was exposed to the women's movement but can't decide where she stands when that movement bucks important Latino traditions regarding her family and community. She wants to maintain her ties to the Latino culture, which puts her at odds with a society that doesn't consider Spanish a legitimate tongue, particularly if spoken in the workplace, but a kind of pig latin used by Latinos as a secret code to ridicule gringos. She seeks equal opportunity but represents one of the lowest-paid segments of the population.

ARE LATINAS EARNING THEIR FAIR SHARE IN THE WORKPLACE?

According to a 1999 Current Population Survey conducted by the Census Bureau, 2.6 percent of Latinas earned $50,000 or more compared to 7.1 percent of non-Hispanic white women. Overall, the earnings of non-Hispanic white women were 17 percent higher than those of African American women and 39 percent higher than earnings for Latinas.

Still, the modern Latina has many more options available to her than her mother or grandmother did. But without their experience in the same situation, she'll be challenged to make the right decision. From careers to boyfriends, the choice is hers, but she'll need to be well informed in order to choose wisely. The point of this book is to help Latinas examine their love choices. To begin with, before she knows what kind of relationship she wants, the modern Latina needs to figure out who she is.

Who is the Modern Latina?

THE DICTIONARY DEFINES modern as "a person of modern times or views." By definition, then, a modern Latina is definitely a woman of the new millennium. She was raised in modern times when the role of women in the United States began to change. But she also comes from a unique cultural background with its own values and traditions. "We are really a different generation," says Sandra Guzman, author of *The Latina Bible.* "I am definitely an American-made woman with all the richness of the Latino culture." For the purpose of this discussion, the modern Latina was born from the late forties through the mid-eighties. She was raised in a household that was both modern and "old world" or colonial in its traditions. Modernity, however, is not only a reflection of the decade in which she was born, but also what generation of American she is. Modern Latinas know that the number of generations that separate us from our Latin roots *really* matters.

So long as the U.S. shares a border with Mexico, immigration from there as well as from Central and South America, the Caribbean, and even Spain, will continue, guaranteeing that a first-generation U.S.

resident who calls herself a Latina is born everyday. Although the decade into which a Latina is born matters, the experience of a first-generation Latina is somewhat unchanged. For example, a first generation Latina who was born in the seventies or eighties was probably not raised in as restrictive an environment as the first generation Latina born in the fifties. Still, a first-generation Latina born today would be raised in a less liberal environment than a fifth or sixth generation Latina born in the same decade. The bottom line here is that the number of generations that separate a Latina from her Latin origins will also distance her from traditional Latino culture and will affect her approach to relationships—that is, whether she will be more or less traditional.

For a first-generation Latina born in the fifties, the appliances were probably the only modern conveniences in the home. The family dynamic had her washing and cooking for her father and brothers alongside her mother and sisters and generally being seen but not heard. The boys were encouraged to grow up, get out of the house, and be men, while the girls were told to be good, get married, and only then leave home. Traditionally, a Latina's career path took her from her father's house to her husband's. On the upside, this Latina probably spoke Spanish at home, which gave her invaluable bilingual skills. Unfortunately, a Spanish speaker of this generation was often persecuted or traumatized in school, which meant she encouraged her own children to speak only English. When it came time to leave home, she probably married a family friend or acquaintance and moved into a home next door, or at least within walking distance from her parents' house.

MIJOS

Did your mother grow up with brothers? If so, ask her about her family dynamic. Did she ever feel slighted by her mother in favor of them? How did it affect her?

For the second or third-generation Latina born in the sixties, she and her brothers may have had to share the dishwashing duties, but when push came to shove, only her brothers were sent to college. Still, being more acclimated to U.S. culture and with English as her first language, this determined Latina made her way through community college or acquired the financial aid to go to a four-year university. Armed with a college education, this Latina was as likely to move back home to find work or to set up a business as she was to move across the country for the same opportunities. She also probably married a Latino who has a similar education, though she may decide to marry a non-Latino. Although her Spanish skills may not be as sharp as she'd like, she will make a big effort to encourage those skills in her children.

Fourth- and fifth-generation Latinas born in the seventies and eighties grew up with respect and pride for their heritage but at a much greater distance from it and, consequently, with fewer culture clashes. In school, they were viewed by their non-Latina classmates as peers, not as outsiders, and they wore the same clothes, read the same magazines, watched the same television shows, and listened to the same music. They received the same treatment as their brothers and were challenged by the same expectations from their parents. They were given as many opportunities and tools for success as their parents could afford. There was never a question of whether they would go to college. The question was where they would go to college and what they would study. They've also taken on more "American" attributes that include greater sexual freedom. These girls are in no hurry to get married.

For Latinas, the college experience is singular. Once they arrive, they find themselves swept up in a cultural revolution, where they have to make some difficult choices. College profoundly affects any young person, but for Latinos (both girls and boys), many of whom are the first in the family to attend college, the experience can be polarizing. Some Latinas find kinship with fellow Latinos. They might join Movimiento Estudiantil Chicano de Aztlán (MEChA) or another Latino student group, march for the United Farm Workers, and embrace other Latino causes.

For other Latinas, the experience has quite the opposite effect. Rather than embrace their culture, they may become estranged from it. Born and raised in a part of the country with a large Latino population, these Latinas experience culture shock when they attend a college with nary a Latino in sight. In an effort to blend in, they learn to disguise rather than celebrate their Latin roots. Suddenly, the prospect of succeeding in a *gringo* world becomes a top priority, and these Latinas focus on their careers and increasing their social clout rather than worrying about their community's visibility. They may not be considered politically correct, but these women are also modern Latinas.

Male and Female Roles

BESIDES HER GENERATION or age, a Latina's approach to love will also be affected by her siblings' gender. For Latinas without brothers, the oldest sister feels the cultural advantages and disadvantages of her generation most keenly. She serves as a role model for her younger siblings, who will watch, learn, and gain a distinct advantage in real world situations from her. When it comes to romance, a big sister will usually test the waters first and offer valuable advice on dating and romance. Parental expectations for girls are also higher without boys in the mix since there is no male hierarchy to respect among the siblings. More significantly, Latinas without brothers will escape the experience of being raised by male-centered moms.

It is an acknowledged truth that many Latina moms are male-centered and tend to raise *mijos*, (men coddled and adored by their mothers). I think the tendency exists in most Latinas but lies dormant until they have sons. My sisters and I were spared, but had we had a brother, our family would have been no different. Both of my grandmothers doted on their sons and grandsons. My parents wanted sons very badly. It didn't happen, but I know that if I had had brothers, I would not be the same person. My mother admits that if she had had sons, my sisters and I would have assumed the traditional roles of females in a Latino family, meaning we would have served the men at dinner, and my brothers would have been exempted from doing household chores. Without brothers, though, my sisters and I grew up educated, independent women. That's not to say that we're perfect or that it's better not to have brothers, but given my family's history, our sense of self may not have been as strong if we had been battered by the constant attention and preferential treatment given to a brother.

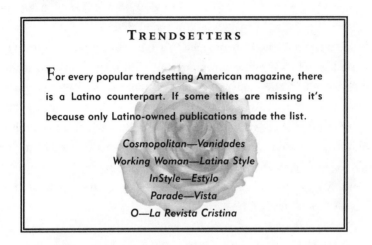

TRENDSETTERS

For every popular trendsetting American magazine, there is a Latino counterpart. If some titles are missing it's because only Latino-owned publications made the list.

Cosmopolitan—Vanidades
Working Woman—Latina Style
InStyle—Estylo
Parade—Vista
O—La Revista Cristina

This male-centeredness is still perpetuated by modern Latinas. I once worked with a woman who had a beautiful little girl. Everyone admired her because she was so pretty, smart, and well mannered. The mother, an educated, professional, and second-generation Latina, claimed that her daughter was the apple of her eye. A few years passed, the mom became pregnant, and this time she bore a son. She admitted to feeling emotions about this child that she never felt for her daughter. The woman was so blown away by her *mijo* that one day she commented, "I'm so crazy about my son that even though I know he'll get married some day, I already hate his wife." For any woman, the key to a successful romance is her level of self-confidence. When a girl gets the distinct impression-that next to her brother she's chopped liver, she too will start to focus on pleasing men and will seek male validation in order to feel good about herself.

Clearly, the modern Latina has to deal with outdated traditions regarding male and female roles. In some cases, she has already overcome them. She's now encouraged to acquire an education. She's self-confident when it comes to interacting with men, even though she tries to hide it. The modern Latina even appreciates being thought of as sexy, sultry, and passionate and she doesn't feel she has to prove it by sleeping with every man she meets. The modern Latina is educated and in some ways, more acculturated rather than assimilated. She has maintained her native culture while adopting many American customs. She reads women's magazines like *Vogue* and *Elle* as well as *Latina Style*, *Estylo*, or *Vanidades*.

American and *Latina*

LATINAS COME FROM all thirty-three countries in Latin America as well as Spain, and bring with them cultural traditions unique to each place. Immigration from some of these countries is heavier than others and the history in the U.S. of some groups is longer, too. For example, Mexican Americans have the longest history in this country, but some may still be first or second generation U.S. citizens. Of late, the greatest boom in immigration has come from Central America. In Los Angeles, El Salvador produced a great number of new immigrants, while in Miami, immigrants from Colombia showed a surge.

LATINOS IN AMERICA

Here is the breakdown of each group from their country of origin regardless of generation:

Mexican: 58.5%
Puerto Rican: 9.6%
Central American: 4.8%
South American: 3.8%
Cuban: 3.5%
All others: 19.8%

Source: The Bureau of the Census 2000 survey
www.census.gov/

Yet, after all is said and done, the modern Latina still feels pressured to be more "American," and this feeling is constantly at odds with the way she was raised. She runs the risk of losing her sense of self and, consequently, her sense of direction. Should she sleep around? Should she be more aggressive at the office? Should she hide her ability to speak Spanish unless asked? Should she swap her red lipstick for a clear glossy look? These questions become more pressing as more Latinas enter the professional world and new generations are born. Despite all their inner confidence, Latinas may still feel like outsiders.

Even so, the U.S. Latino population continues to grow. From 1990 to 2000, the Latino population increased by nearly 60 percent (from 22.4 million to 35.3 million), more than any other group. Some may find that figure alarming, but reports about the "browning of

America" are exaggerated—at 12.5 percent, Latinos still make up just a fraction of the total population. In areas where the Latino population is strong, like Miami, San Antonio, Los Angeles, New York, or Chicago, Latinas will inevitably find other Latinas in the workplace who can provide a support group. But Latinas in Iowa, Minnesota, or Delaware may not be so lucky, and the urge to blend in rather than stick out can be overwhelming. Latinas are not immune to feelings of insecurity or self-doubt; and when culturally isolated, they feel challenged.

Another important component of the modern Latina is history. Modern Latinas carry the five hundred-year-history of Latinas in North America in their hearts. That history includes enduring and overcoming one stereotype after another. For many years, Latinas were considered passive and subservient slaves to the whims of their macho husbands. While this stereotype may be based on a cultural truth, the entertainment industry hyper-inflated this image. As the television and film industries developed, these stereotypes also evolved. In Hollywood, Latinas were first seen as passive maids, then viewed as oversexed, hot-blooded spitfires, which left them only two roles to play: seductress or maid. In the 1960s, Academy Award-winning actress Rita Moreno left the movie industry for seven years rather than play the same role over and over. She remembers how quickly she became typecast, and was even dubbed "Rita the Cheetah," by the press. "One reporter claimed I had a necklace made from the teeth of my boyfriends," she says in Luis Reyes's *Hispanics in Hollywood*, "so with an image like that I wasn't offered many passive or interesting parts." True to her nature, and that of the modern Latina, Rita persevered and eventually laid a path for young Latina actresses to follow.

Latinas in Hollywood still experience the same problems Moreno faced more than thirty years ago, but the image of Latinas has become more mainstream and opportunities in the film industry have opened up a bit. Actresses like Jennifer Lopez, Salma Hayek, Cameron Diaz, and Penelope Cruz have all emerged to play both Latinas and non-Latina roles in independent films and Hollywood blockbusters. Like all stereotypes, the images of Latinas as maids or spitfires were born out of ignorance and have been dispelled, over time and through education. Still, change is slow going, and the number of high-profile Latinas in Hollywood remains small.

Unlike the stereotype, Latinas are generally coy when it comes to sex. Coyness is an inherited cultural behavior that the modern Latina has not abandoned and which she still uses to mask her confidence. Raised not to show off or brag, Latinas place a great emphasis on gentility, poise, and etiquette. Old-world traditions taught Latinas to be seen but not heard, and although that jaded idea has faded, Latinas are still taught to practice tact and discretion in mixed company. Many Latinas take the demure approach when it comes to sex and reveal their sexuality through casual flirting as opposed to casual sex. For Latinas, flirting isn't the sign of loose morals; it just comes naturally and can be a lot of fun. And though today's average Latina is naturally sensual and as open to suggestion as the next girl is, depending on the generation, she may still have to contend with her mother's provincial attitude toward sex.

LATINAS IN LOVE SURVEY

Q: At what age did you lose your virginity?

A: The majority of Latinas surveyed said that they lost their virginity between the ages of eighteen and nineteen.

In addition, she can be downright conceited when it comes to her sex appeal. Many Latinas gladly boast that, in general, they are good-looking people who men find appealing. The Latina body type has never fit in with the long-legged, bookmark-thin model paradigm, but Latinas know that the joke is on these diet-crazy women. Although she certainly has her fans, *Ally McBeal's* Calista "Flaca" Flockhart cannot compete as a sex symbol next to Salma Hayek. Yet for many women, looking like Ally McBeal is a dieting goal! For many Latinas, however, the healthy, athletic figures of Salma Hayek, Jennifer Lopez, and Daisy Fuentes are more admired. Playwright Josefina Lopez captured this attitude best in the title of her play *Real Women Have Curves*. The movie version of the play won an Audience Award at the 2002 Sundance Film Festival. Evidently, the Latina playwright struck a chord.

That's not to say that some Latinas don't suffer from low self-esteem, occasionally (especially in the political or professional context), or that they don't struggle with weight issues, but in the battle of the sexes, Latinas can get loud and proud. They don't just feel pretty; they know they have physical attributes that men want—curves. Jennifer Lopez continually boasts about her well-endowed backside, even though she did hire a trainer to trim it down a bit. Supermodel Cindy Crawford responded with a left-handed compliment, saying she admired Lopez's confidence but wouldn't have the guts to go out in public with an ass that size—or words to that effect. Jennifer remains undaunted and Latinas love her for it.

The modern Latina celebrates her femininity. She exults in knowing that if she wants to bring a man to his knees, she can. This Latina pays attention to her appearance and can become quite an expert at that "put together" look—rich or poor, a Latina will always look as good as she can before going out in public. Again, this is where Latinas split from the women's movement. A feminist would never consider using her feminine charms in any situation, but Latinas see themselves as completely and totally female and are proud of it. In romance, a modern Latina does not deliberately use her sexuality; it's more of a subconscious act. Latinas have an innate duality inherited from the culture clash from which they emerged, so, as tempting as it might be to use her sexuality for her own ends, the modern Latina shies away from overdoing it. For the modern Latina, it's enough to know that when she walks into a room, she will turn a head or two. She's comfortable in her female skin, and that confidence is engaging.

What We Want

THERE IS STILL so much more left for the world to learn about Latinas. For instance, the Latino family structure is matriarchal. Historically, women—moms, grandmothers, sisters, and aunts—ruled the family, gently but firmly and in some cases, very quietly. For all their bluster, Latino men have traditionally left most of the child-rearing and domestic decisions to their wives. In the modern Latino household, Latinas still rule the family but many of them also have careers, and they're much more vocal about their needs, beliefs, and desires. The modern Latina still appreciates the position she holds in the family unit, but she wants some muscle to back it up.

Latinas also share a very special bond with their mothers. Even though my grandmother clearly favored the men in the family, my mother and her sisters adored their mother. Many successful Latinas name their mother or grandmother as their role model. These women have been strong and loving to their children and grandchildren. The Latino family depends on mothers, sisters, aunts, and grandmothers—they are considered the glue that binds the family together. Latinas do indeed hold a powerful position in the family. However, as writer Ana Castillo once told me, "There's a difference between being strong and being in power. Our mothers were able to take a lot, they endured, but that doesn't mean that they were empowered." The modern Latina strives for both strength and empowerment. She wants to maintain her position as the center of the family, but she also wants credit for her work and a partner who will help rather than hinder her. According to the 2000 U.S. Census, Latina entrepreneurs are one of the fastest growing groups of business owners in the country. This means that Latinas who are looking for financial independence will need partners who can respect and support their goals.

Latina history in the U.S. is about accomplishment in all areas of life. Latinas have blazed a trail in their respective fields. In 1966, Dolores

Huerta teamed up with Cesar Chavez to form the United Farm Workers union. Also in the 1960s, Dr. Antonia Pantoja, alarmed at rising high school dropout rates among Puerto Ricans in New York, helped establish ASPIRA, a national nonprofit organization that promotes youth leadership and education. In 1989, Cubana Ileana Ros-Lehtinen ran for the U.S. House of Representatives in a special election to fill a vacancy in Florida and became the first Latina to serve in Congress. In the nineties, Linda Alvarado became the first Hispanic professional team owner (she co-owns the Colorado Rockies), and Linda Chavez-Thompson was voted the vice president of the AFL-CIO, becoming the highest-ranking Latino or woman in the largest labor union in the country.

LATINAS IN BUSINESS

Latina entrepreneurs are one of the fastest growing groups of business owners in the country. The number of Latino/a-owned businesses reached 1.2 million in 1997.

Source: 2000 U.S. Census

With these women and many more as role models, the modern Latina grew up with the women's movement, but the tenets of the movement surrounded rather than possessed her. She appreciated the struggle for equality and the desire to earn equal pay for equal work, but women like Gloria Steinem and Betty Friedan didn't speak directly to her, so she reconfigured the movement to suit her needs. Latinas support the concepts of equality but not the historical approach. The modern Latina clings to her femininity even when she's surrounded by upwardly mobile non-Latinas at the office who have accepted the dogma that in order for a woman to succeed, she has to think, dress, and act like a man. The modern Latina just doesn't own a closet full of black suits and gray and white shirts. She's got to have a fuscia something in her closet or purse, even it's just a belt or a scarf or a lipstick. Most Latinas don't want to blend in, although many are sorely tempted. They want to be appreciated for their individuality, and one way in which it's expressed is in their personal style.

Latinas are grateful for the strides made by the women's movement. Still, the women's movement has been as discomfiting as it's been helpful. While it encouraged women to fight for equality, it also encouraged them to sacrifice their femininity, and not just in the workplace. The early leaders of the women's movement were educated, affluent, Anglo women who delivered a universal message, but without a universal voice. Women of color, then and now, are rarely seen in the upper echelons of the National Organization for Women, which is what gives a political movement a universal voice. When asked if they support the women's movement, a majority of the Latinas in the Latinas in Love survey said, "Absolutely." But many also felt that the movement did not include women of color. "They have not done as good a job as they could and when they do reach out, it's usually to African American women," said one forty-something Latina from Los Angeles when asked if the women's movement has included women of color. Another thirty-something Latina in Texas wrote: "In my opinion, no. Non-Latina women have only reached out to each other (i.e., Anglos and African Americans) and seem to think Latinas don't need to be liberated."

Generally speaking, Latinas have embraced the ideas of the women's movement, and so their approach toward relationships has been altered, along with that of every other "liberated" woman. The women's movement encouraged women to seek equality in the office as well as in the bedroom. Women were encouraged to get in touch with their sexuality, to abandon paternalistic values that placed a high cachet on virginity for women but not for men, and to demand the right to have an orgasm. If men could sow their wild oats, why couldn't women? Latinas have not quite made that leap, but they have managed to move away from the Madonna/whore paradigm (i.e. good girls are for marrying and bad girls are for sex) imposed upon them as girls and have developed greater expectations from their mates as husbands, fathers, and lovers. In their unique way, Latinas have found a middle ground that allows them to maintain their femininity while increasing their clout. The modern Latina still looks for love, but she's also looking for a partner. She wants to be on equal terms with her husband, not pigeon-holed in the role of wife and mother, and she may choose a man who respects her desire for equality over a man who keeps her titillated. Of course, if she can find a man who does both, so much the better.

A Latina wants what all women want—to be loved. But she also wants a partner and a man who can respect her independence. She also wants romance and to be excited by love. She needs a man who will respect her culture and not require that she hide her true identity. But what the modern Latina should know, if she hasn't already come to this conclusion, is that she should never deny her true self. When a Latina tries to be more like someone else and less like herself, she gets into trouble. The modern Latina should know that it's okay to be sexy or to wear jewelry with a business suit. She needs to continue to move forward and behave with class and dignity. She needs to be sure who she is and what she wants. Latinas should be loud and proud both personally and politically. This will give voice to the millions of Latinas who need a women's movement that reflects their agenda. The remaining chapters of this book will look at separate aspects of love for Latinas, with the emphasis on our self-awareness. Remember, we are in vogue, and brown (from *café negro* to *café con leche*) is beautiful!

2

Our Mothers' Daughters

*What mothers tell their daughters shapes
their lives forever*

Dear Pilar,

I'm so grateful that my mom gave me great lessons about
life. She always taught me to respect myself and to be confident. However, several of my friends had moms who didn't
encourage them, and I see them making really bad choices.
How can I help my friends or is it too late?

Anna, 28

ANNA'S LETTER POINTS out a common feeling Latinas
have about their mothers' advice. While the advice is valuable, sometimes mothers say the strangest things. Whether they know
it or not, their daughters are listening. According to results of the
National Longitudinal Study of Adolescent Health released in 2002,
teens who feel close to their mothers are more likely to follow their

mom's advice, especially about sex. All mothers share a special bond with their children, but Latina daughters try to emulate the most important female role model in their lives—their *madres*.

We remember the early lessons our mothers taught us, like being polite to elders, speaking only when spoken to, or being seen but not heard. These lessons are droned into us from an early age because they support the Old World Latino attitude about a woman's place in society, which according to many mothers and grandmothers, should still be the home. Despite the fact that today's Latinas—from secretaries to CEOs—are very much a part of the workforce, young Latinas are still raised to be obedient, modest, and demure. That doesn't mean they're raised to be subservient, although many of them tend to be compliant. On the contrary, these traits have been stressed not just because our mothers were brought up that way but also because it's believed that they will instill elegance, respectfulness, and dignity in us as we grow older.

TOP FIVE DICHOS EN MI FAMILIA

1. *El amor de lejos es de p****jos*—Long-distance love is for idiots.

2. *Mejor sola que mal acompañada*—It's better to be alone than in bad company.

3. *La suerte de la fea la bonita lo desea*—The luck of the plain girl, the pretty girl envies.

4. *Lo que no mata engorda*—What doesn't kill you makes you fat.

5. *No hay mal que por bien no venga*—Every cloud has a silver lining.

These are the big lessons Latinas are taught by their mothers, but even little lessons, or what may have seemed like scolding at the time, have an impact. Cleaning our room, taking care of our siblings, or keeping the hair out of our face are all little reminders of what girls need to know to be successful women. "You have such a pretty face, why do you keep hiding it?" my mother used to ask me as she pulled my hair back into a tight ponytail. The youngest of three girls, I was a tomboy and I liked to play outside. Naturally, my ponytail or pigtails would come loose and my hair would hang in my face. It seemed like such an insignificant thing to focus on and to have to stop what I was doing to fix. Still, the fact that my mother told me repeatedly that I was pretty was definitely a good thing. She may just have wanted me to look neat, but on some level it sunk in and helped sustain my budding but fragile self-confidence.

From the moment children are born, they are influenced by their mother more than any other person. We remember the things our mothers did and said that had an impact in our lives. Not only do young Latinas listen to what their mothers say; they also model themselves after what they do. For their daughters, mothers have many important lessons to impart about how to be successful wives, mothers, sisters, aunts, lovers, professionals, and entrepreneurs. Most importantly, mothers impart confidence and pride in their daughters and teach them about self-esteem. "Self-esteem is *la fuerza potente,* the powerful force within yourself that is capable of enabling you to realize your fullest potential as a human being," write Rosa Maria Gil and Carmen Inoa Vazquez in *The Maria Paradox.* "Let us assure you that without a solid, positive self-esteem, you will be substantially limiting your chances of achieving your goals."

Latinas will be as individual and talented as their mothers train them to be. Of course, the sins of the mother are also passed down through the generations, so Latinos aren't just learning from their moms, but also their grandmothers and even great grandmothers, and these lessons are good as well as bad. Accordingly, Latinas need to step back and assess the good, the bad, and the ugly about their tradition and culture, many times reinforced by their moms and grandmoms, and decide whether to discard these lessons or modify them to fit their modern lives.

• LESSON 1 •

Speak Only When Spoken To

WHEN YOUNG LATINAS are told to be quiet or not to speak unless spoken to, they learn several things. On one hand, they learn to listen attentively, to be polite, and to be respectful of a person's opinion. But when this sentence is used as a reproach, children also learn that their opinions don't matter, that they are not equal participants in the conversation, and that there is a hierarchy in place that puts adults above children, and in some cases boys above girls. Some aspects of this lesson are definitely keepers, but as a whole, this statement needs to be modified to work effectively in modern times.

Teaching children to respect their elders is a good thing. This seems like pretty basic stuff, but the theories about how we should raise children today have drastically changed from the days when many Latina mothers were children. As a result, modern Latino parents not only question the lessons they learned from their own mothers and fathers, but also the validity of their own judgment. They are much more careful to encourage their child to be an individual, to let his or her personality develop on its own rather than mold it, and to nurture their child's innate talents as they begin to emerge. Since the objective is to build a child's self-confidence, this approach is hard to argue with. But teaching a child to listen is always beneficial and will serve her well in adulthood. Children's thoughts and opinions are constantly growing and changing, and they still have much to learn. By respecting elders and listening and learning from their stories and example, children can avoid some common mistakes and grow up to be respected and successful adults.

This rule also gives kids parameters within the family unit. Most parenting books encourage parents to give children structure and say that the basic hierarchy of adults over children is correct. My mother continually discouraged me from joining in the conversations she had with her friends, sometimes successfully but usually not. I loved to listen to her gossip with my aunts or her close friends, but I was also a small child with a big mouth. More than once I embarrassed my mother by blabbing the gossip by accident. Finally, my mother banned me from listening to adult discourse. Until I could appreciate the sanctity of private adult conversations, I was relegated to playing outside with the rest of the kids. Since I had proven that I couldn't keep a secret, I had to earn my way back by learning to keep quiet. There was no value judgment here. My mother's sanction didn't make me feel like a lesser person. It just made me want to get it right so that I would be invited back.

Still, the speak-only-when-spoken-to lesson needs some work. First and foremost, it has to be expanded to include boys as well. The fact that girls are raised differently in Latino families than boys is, unfortunately, not a myth. In *Dr. Ana Nogales' Book of Love, Sex, and Relationships,* she refers to this dichotomy, asking: "Should we give our daughters the same kind of encouragement and advice we give to our sons—or is Latino culture correct in making greater distinctions between the sexes?" We all know the answer to this question. But Latinas also know that until quite recently, girls were not given the same encouragement or advice as their brothers. Girls paid a much higher price for being rude, loud, or interrupting conversations than boys did. In the past, boys were encouraged to run around and make a racket, so long as they did it outside. But even when they acted like their little loud selves in the house and interrupted adult conversations, they were rarely scolded or punished. Girls, who tend to want to interact with adults more than boys, were often stifled from participating in conversations, making them feel less important.

If used wisely, the speak-only-when-spoken-to lesson can be a great tool that teaches children not to monopolize a conversation or constantly interrupt people. Still, Latina moms must be careful—there's a fine line between teaching their daughters to be polite while instilling confidence in their ability to express themselves and teaching them that their feelings and opinions aren't important.

Modern Lesson: It's impolite to interrupt, so be respectful when participating in conversations.

• LESSON 2 •

Look Good, Be Thin, and Don't Talk Back or You'll Never Get a Man

ACTRESS JOANNA LUMLEY, who portrays the tragically hip Patsy Stone on the brilliant British comedy *Absolutely Fabulous*, once said, "Women are very anxious people" during a television interview. That kind of sums it up for me. We all worry about our hair, our weight, our skin, our bikini lines, our wrinkles, our cellulite, our butts, our breast size, our everything! This lesson clearly reinforces all of this bad juju. Whatever well-meaning advice this lesson was meant to impart has been buried over the years under images of pencil thin women with big artificially enlarged breasts. The fact is, though, looks *do* matter. Almost every species uses looks to attract a mate, but in American society, the concept of ideal beauty does not reflect the reality that the average-sized woman in this country is a size fourteen. Since women need to ease rather than heighten their anxiety about their looks, this lesson needs serious retooling.

Latina mothers always stress looks with their daughters. I had acne as a teenager, and when I resisted going to a dermatologist my mother would persuade me with one line, "Remember, your face is your fortune." I was called *gordita* or "tubby" even though I weighed between 105 and 110 pounds in high school and through college. I have friends whose mothers badgered them daily about dieting and even ridiculed them for eating pumpkin pie at Thanksgiving. Consequently, Latinas are very mindful of their appearance and take great pride in perfecting their skills at putting on makeup and choosing the right ensemble. The basic lesson of good grooming is not a bad one. Indeed, lessons and lectures from Latina mothers stressing appearance may start out as an exercise in building self-confidence: If you take pride in your appearance, people will respect you, and being treated with respect by other people naturally boosts self-esteem. Well sure, but we're not supposed to care what other people think, right?

The fact that good grooming is important because it's a reflection of personal pride and confidence is about all that's good about this lesson. When we dress to impress other people, we chip away at the positive self-image we've worked so hard to build. "We must mention here that your self-esteem can never depend only on others' opinions, because that gives outsiders control over your actions, values, and attitudes," write Gil and Vazquez. "If you allow that to happen, you'll live in anguish, depending *en el que dirán*, on what others say about you." Women should dress for themselves so that when they look in the mirror, they like what they see. We all know that in order to pull off any look or style, you have to have the right attitude. The same goes for feeling good about yourself—you need the right attitude. The way in which people react to you will reinforce, not create, your confidence. Anything genuine impresses people, and when you feel good about yourself, you exude genuine confidence.

Being thin is another thing Latina mothers like to dwell on. Of course it's important for everyone to strive for good health, which requires exercise and a balanced diet, and thinness is the likely result. In fact, maintaining a healthy lifestyle is even more important for Latinos, who are twice as likely to develop type 2 diabetes, a condition associated with a poor diet, lack of exercise, and obesity. Latinos are also at great risk for heart disease and stroke, which are the number-one causes of death in our community. But obsessive dieting based on a poor body image never works and usually just escalates into dangerous disorders like bulimia or anorexia. Latinas have natural curves, and if that means we lean more toward *llenita* than *flacita*, so be it.

Unfortunately, there's much more buried in this lesson than just looking good and being thin. It also implies that we always have to be nice and accommodating if we want to land a boyfriend or husband, which is absolutely not true. If looking good to impress others is wrong—remember, we have to build our own self-esteem—then doing the same to get a man doesn't work either. In fact, this message may be at the root of our anxiety as Latin women. This way of thinking encourages Latinas to objectify themselves rather than get to know and love themselves. In other words, it teaches a girl that she's not worthy, that her opinions don't matter, that she doesn't have the right to defend herself, and that her value as a human being is determined by her attractiveness to the opposite sex.

In the shadow of the women's movement, it is shocking that Latina mothers still teach their daughters this dysfunctional lesson, but many may be doing it unconsciously. The lesson usually comes from a certain type of Latina, one who was raised in a "male-centered" household. Regardless of how modern they think they are, many Latinas still buy into this notion, just like their mothers and grandmothers did. This lesson was clearly hatched from an Old World, male-centered way of thinking. Gil and Vazquez refer to this mindset as *Marianismo*, whereby respect and worship of the Virgin Mary by Latinos is carried over onto the role of women, which is considered a kind of saintly servitude. "*Marianismo* is about sacred duty, self-sacrifice, and chastity. About dispensing care and pleasure, but not receiving them. About living in the shadows, literally and figuratively, of your men—father, boyfriend, husband, son—your kids, your family," they write. Becoming invisible is not healthy for anyone's psyche. All women like a little flattery and male attention. There's nothing wrong with wanting to be desired; in fact, husbands should take note that making their wives feel desirable is an essential ingredient for domestic bliss. But when a woman needs a man's approval so much that she will subjugate her own needs and do things she might not normally do just to get that approval, she has a problem. Many times, however, male-centered women will not be conscious of what they're doing and will vehemently deny the truth when challenged. Some may claim to be feminists, yet in their personal lives, they live to please their man. If these Latinas have daughters, they'll pick up the message quickly.

They'll notice the different tone of voice their mom uses when speaking to them as opposed to their brothers. They'll notice the genuine affection their mom expresses to their brothers while she criticizes the daughters for being too fat or not putting on makeup. If they don't have brothers, these girls will see how their mothers react to their fathers, and that includes accepting a certain level of abuse. These moms will focus on pleasing their husbands first, which means making sure that the kids please Daddy as well. Male-centered women must recognize this condition and then make a conscious effort to fight it. If they don't, they will fail to give their daughters a proper sense of themselves as viable, important people.

LATINOS IN LOVE SURVEY
Is your husband a mamma's boy?

Sixty-two percent said that their husbands were not mama's boys, 19 percent had no answer, 14 percent said yes, and one Latina responded, "He was."

Now, can a woman be boy crazy and not male-centered? Of course! Boy crazy just means she loves boys, and that usually manifests itself in a tendency to flirt or get a little giddy around the opposite sex and generally amounts to harmless fun. In a group of Latinas out on the town, the boy crazy ones will do a lot of flirting and engage in comparison games of the men at the bar. If it escalates at all, with the help of tequila shots or *algo así*, the boy crazy Latina may get loud, but not obnoxious. Being male-centered is more insidious, and the girl with this condition might get desperate toward the end of the evening. Since these women judge themselves based on how men perceive them rather than establishing their own self-esteem, they may get resentful if they're not paid enough attention. Indeed, many male-centered women might exhibit a love-hate attitude toward men, frustrated by their need to be noticed and their inability to make it happen all the time.

These girls are taught to focus on finding a mate. Their mothers probably dwelled on things like weight and appearance and spent most of their time trying to please their own mate while showing less affection and attention to their daughters. This will invariably take its toll on a Latina's self image. By teaching their daughters that they must act and look a certain way to attract men, Latina mothers also teach them to seek male validation at all costs. This determined search for men's approval often overshadows their own personal needs and desires.

I think this is really the worst lesson a Latina mother can teach her daughter. It's one thing to encourage a girl to take pride in how she looks, but it's quite another to teach her that if she's not attractive she'll never snag a man and to advise her to censor her thoughts and feelings just to make sure he sticks around. Building a child's self confidence is essential to his or her success as an adult. A mother should focus on developing her daughter's identity, self-awareness, and sense of style and encourage her to feel good about herself, no matter what other people think. Self-doubt makes us stumble through most decisions in life, and makes us rely on the opinions and approval of others because we can't trust ourselves to make the right decisions. If a Latina in love cannot trust that inner voice that will raise a red flag when a guy says the wrong thing or acts inappropriately, she's basically stuck in the Tunnel of Love, afloat but without a paddle, in the dark, just waiting for a guy, any guy, to come along and save her.

Luckily, not all Latinas are raised this way. My mother always told me to respect myself and not to take shit from any man. However, I'm still surprised by the number of Latina women I know who are shocked and envious when they hear me say this.

The modern version of this lesson should be: Look good, feel great, and love yourself.

LATINAS IN LOVE SURVEY

What's the best advice your mother ever gave you about dating?

"Put a dime between your knees."

"Always look and act like a lady."

"Never let a boy go to your bedroom alone in my house."

"Date and have many friends but don't be sexual, 'Cross your legs, mija.'"

What's the worst advice your mother ever gave you about dating?

"You're not going to find a 'perfect' fit."

"Only bring home guys that your *tios* will like."

"Date a successful man with money because marriage is no picnic so you might as well live comfortably."

"All men are dogs" (men only want one thing).

· LESSON 3 ·

Your Husband Is Always Right

THIS "WINNER" NATURALLY derives from the same source as Lesson 2—male-centered women—and Old World ideas. I wish this lesson were a thing of the past, but unfortunately, a number of women I've spoken with actually said this advice was the worst they had received from their mothers. It was more common among first-generation Latinas, and since they listed it as the "worst" advice, hopefully it won't be repeated to their daughters. This pearl of wisdom is degrading to women and just doesn't work in today's society.

LATINAS IN LOVE SURVEY

What is the best advice your mother ever gave you about marriage?

"She always told me that I need to make sure that I really love and understand the guy I'm going to marry, and that I understand his virtues and defects."

"Once is enough."

"Be yourself from the beginning. Have your husband help with everything around the house from day one and don't let him get into the habit of 'This is her job' type of attitude."

"I don't want to hear about every fight because you'll make up but I'll still be mad."

What is the worst advice your mother ever gave you about marriage?

"At least you won't be alone."

"The honeymoon will be over after a year."

"Obey your husband."

"He has to be Catholic and Hispanic if you're going to marry him."

In a contemporary marriage, husbands and wives are partners. They share everything; chores, responsibilities, finances, childrearing. As equals, the modern couple doesn't see their partner as superior or inferior. They've come together to build a life and they have mutually agreed-upon goals for what they want that life to be. In the past, sex and money issues were the two greatest problems a couple faced and the most common catalysts for infidelity and divorce. Today time, or the lack of it, is certainly a third factor. The modern couple is a working couple, and although that usually solves the money issue, their free time is greatly diminished, which often has a detrimental effect on their sex life that can lead to the couple growing apart. Arguments between husbands and wives today may not be easier to solve but as breadwinners and partners, communication needs to improve so that when problems arise, they can be discussed and worked out. However, if a Latina adopts the attitude that her husband is always right, her marriage is not a partnership; for all intents and purposes, she becomes an indentured servant.

While debunking this lesson is crucial to a Latina's happiness, we should remember that husbands are not always wrong, either. You need to find a balance in your relationship and figure out productive and healthy ways to argue. Throwing a shoe at him, for example, is a bad way to make a point in an argument, as is losing control and screaming. Pilar advises: Listen attentively to what each other has to say and try to see things from the other's perspective. This can cut down drastically on your fights. Keep lines of communication open. To do this, both partners must feel that their opinions are respected and will be heard.

LATINAS IN LOVE SURVEY

When asked to rank the following components of a good marriage—love, money, children, communication, equality, sex, honesty, humor, tenderness, romance, excitement, and compatibility—communication was ranked number two.

To encourage girls to agree rather than argue with husbands harks back to a time when Latina women actually risked physical and financial retaliation from their husbands if they didn't go along with everything the husband wanted. Unfortunately, domestic violence is not a thing of the past, but it is also no longer the norm in a Latino household. To continue to offer this advice reinforces the notion that women must be compliant to keep men happy, and in some cases, as a means of survival. There's nothing salvageable here. Let's forget this lesson and replace it with a new one.

The modern version of this lesson should be: Marry a man who loves you, respects you, and sees you as an equal.

• LESSON 4 •

You've Got To Love Yourself Before You Can Love Someone Else

HOW SUCCESSFUL WE are as Latinas depends on the most important lesson of all—learning to love ourselves. From a lucrative career to a rewarding relationship, self-confidence is the key ingredient. The most successful entrepreneurs always attribute their accomplishments to a combination of factors, but most importantly to a strong belief in themselves that gave them the confidence they needed to take risks. This lesson is not only a keeper, but it builds on Lesson 2, which teaches self-confidence. To use Lesson 4 effectively, Latinas need to say it *con safos* (like they really mean it) to their daughters and believe it themselves. A mother's effectiveness in instilling confidence can mean the difference between success and failure. Of all the lessons a mother will teach, the most important one of all is self-respect or self-love, which invariably leads to self-confidence.

My mother sent my sisters and me to Catholic school from first grade through the end of high school. She had to work the whole time in order to supplement the family income so that my parents could afford the extra expense. She did it, she says, to ensure that we received a religious as well as an academic education. *Pues madre.* As a fourth grader, I had my own group of friends, but I wouldn't say I hung out with the popular crowd. I was second- or third-tier popular. There was a girl, Diana, in the first tier group, who was destined for bitchiness. She could be a bully at times, and one day she decided to make me her next target. She came out of nowhere and suddenly slapped me. I was shocked and did nothing. When I told my mother, she said, "You go back tomorrow and you slap her back. Don't let her get away with that."

Filled with dread, I waited all day to complete my mother's order. I really didn't want to do it; it seemed useless, like I was a day late and a dollar short. After school, I approached her and said, "This is for yesterday," but when I tried to deliver the blow, she ran off. A chase ensued but luckily my oldest sister, who was in the eighth grade, cornered *la cabrona* and held her. I slapped her, twice. I must admit, it felt great, and much to my surprise Diana and I actually became friends. Perhaps she realized the error of her ways, or maybe I scared her, but I think we both realized that we never meant to hurt each other, and once that was out of the way, we could relax and just be friends. This lesson didn't encourage me to fight; I hate fights and have never gotten into another one. It taught me that I should not allow anyone to violate my humanity and that I was worth defending. Afterward, I did feel very proud of myself. Most importantly, I could report to my mother, "Mission accomplished."

MOTHERLY ADVICE

What did your mother tell you about sex and relationships? Ask your mother what she was told by your grandmother and see if you can identify the advice and beliefs your mother decided not to pass on to you.

Encouraging girls to love themselves also gets them to think about themselves, about who they are as individuals, what their likes and dislikes are, what they're looking for in an ideal mate, and what behavior, characteristics, and flaws they will put up with in that mate. For many Latinas, this may seem sinfully selfish, especially to those raised to be nice and compliant, but it's important. Latinas need to be a little self-centered in order to find out who they are—as women, as Latinas, as individuals. If you find this difficult, think of yourself in the third person. If you could be the ideal you, what would you do, where would you live, who would you love? As you discover what the ideal you would be like, try working toward those ideals, one at a time, in your real life. Only through self-discovery can we truly learn to love ourselves.

Our self-image profoundly affects our relationships. Women who are taught to respect themselves, not to settle, and not to take abuse, will become self-assured. Successful women credit their mothers for making them feel that they could achieve all their goals and aspirations. Confidence also sustains women as they rebound from broken love relationships. The more you know about yourself, the easier it will be to spot Mr. Wrong, especially before things go too far and you start convincing yourself that Mr. Wrong may be Mr. Right. If the only lesson Latinas learn from their mothers about men is that they need to do whatever they have to do get him, from dieting to keeping silent, then their chances of finding a good relationship are doomed. If instead they learn that they are beautiful—inside and out—and that the guy who sees that is Mr. Right, they will have a good chance of finding true love. That's not to say that confident woman don't get their hearts broken, but they do rebound faster and more importantly, they learn something from each experience.

Loving yourself takes patience and diligence. We are all struck by insecurities, but if we truly love ourselves unconditionally, with all our faults as well as virtues, we can work through them. With this valuable lesson, we can find the right romantic partner, someone who loves us unconditionally. If Latinas learn to defend, respect, and believe in themselves from their mothers early on, they will mature into the confident Latinas they need to be to give and receive love well.

Modern Lesson: This lesson is timeless.

• LESSON 5 •

Why Buy the Cow When You Can Get the Milk for Free?

SOME LESSONS ARE more important than others and for these, Latina mothers rely on proverbs, old wives tales, *dichos*, the church, or any other kind of higher authority to emphasize their importance. One lesson, among the oldest and the most universal, is, "Don't have sex until you get married because a guy will never buy the cow if he's getting the milk for free."

Even in the wake of the women's movement, mothers still don't want their daughters to be perceived as "easy." Although they may have accepted that a woman has a right to an orgasm, they still won't talk about it. They definitely will not encourage their daughters to masturbate, even though many sex educators, including the phenomenal Sue Johansen, host of the Canadian weekly program *The Sunday Night Sex Show* and Dr. Ana Nogales, author of *Dr. Ana Nogales' Book of Love, Sex, and Relationships*, assert that masturbation helps women discover what feels good and how to recognize their own orgasm. "I often suggest to women that they explore their own bodies, to discover all the areas that are arousing to them," writes Nogales. "I also like to suggest that women look at their genital area because this part of our body is hidden from our eyes. . . . She can also look at her entire body, not to see if she has more fat than she would like or to compare herself to other women but just to look at how nature has made her own body so unique."

At a time when sex has permeated almost all facets of life to the point of being blown out of proportion, this lesson, where the cow and the milk are virginal commodities, seems woefully outdated and irrelevant. Sex is everywhere, from hip-hugging jeans to Viagra. How could a show like *Sex and the City*, where all four female characters are fairly promiscuous, be so popular if women didn't secretly wish that they could be as sexually guilt-free as these make-believe females are? The show strikes that chord in women, but it also brings to light women's general angst when it comes to relationships. In my opinion, the best part of the show is when the characters talk about relationships and how to make them work. Miranda is having a baby out of wedlock, Charlotte is getting divorced, Carrie let go of the ideal boyfriend and is unable to free herself from her commitment-phobic ex-boyfriend Mr. Big, and Samantha, the most sexually liberated, who argues against relationships in general, has fallen in love. These plot lines explain the show's popularity among women, but since it's a cable show on HBO it's fair to assume that men are watching as well. They tune in to see the scantily clad Carrie Bradshaw, the show's lead character, and the usually-naked-and-in-bed Samantha Jones. Clearly, on television, Lesson 5 could never be applied because nobody would want to watch the show. In the real world, however, new research shows that there may be some substance to this lesson.

In her book, *Getting to "I Do,"* psychologist Patricia Allen reveals that a woman's inability to disconnect her head from her vagina is not simply a social affliction, it's biological. The culprit is a hormone called oxytocin and causes a mental bond. In childbirth, while breast-feeding, and during an orgasm women produce oxytocin, in larger quantities than men. No matter how casually the relationship begins, over time, a woman will form an attachment to her lover. "Soon the sound of his voice, the look on his face, the touch of his hands becomes intensely associated with the addictive pleasure that oxytocin brings," Allen explains.

For years, women have struggled to achieve sexual liberation but without complete success. Women have learned to demand equal pleasure in bed, to switch mating roles and ask a guy out on a date, or go to a club specifically looking for a one-night stand. They've heard *The Vagina Monologues, en inglés y en español,* but for some reason, women seem to hit the same wall when it comes to romance. One thirty-something Latina revealed to me that she was not a prude at all when it came to sex, but she was troubled by a recent relationship that went sour. She met a man through friends and they immediately connected. He asked her to go home with him that night, but she refused. They dated a couple more times, and once they did have sex, he stopped calling. They saw each other one more time, but he broke it off with her shortly after that. This girl was experienced, so she didn't think that the sex was the problem. So if she had gotten the sex part right, why did he dump her? Basically, she was outwitted by oxytocin. For his part, the guy wanted to go home with her after meeting her for the first time, so clearly that's all he wanted. Skilled at the art of seduction, he poured on the charm and led her to believe that he was attracted to her as a person, not as an object. Once he got what he wanted, he left. But this Latina was baffled. She thought that being sexually free meant she was more sophisticated and therefore better equipped to sustain a modern romance. The problem is, she's still a girl and although she's intellectualized her sexuality and put her theories into action, her heart, with the help of oxytocin, is telling her she wants to be loved.

Originally, this lesson was intended to keep women virgins until they got married because they were commodities and had to remain unspoiled goods. In modern times, it serves to keep girls from becoming promiscuous and to discourage them from "shacking up." According to Naomi Wolf, author of *Promiscuities,* virginal women and promiscuous women have been pitted against each other. The women's movement encouraged women to break free from male dominance in the boardroom and the bedroom, but it didn't give the next generation of young women, who would be more sexually active than their mothers, any new rules. Is there such a thing as too much sex? Can women be sexually free but only in moderation? According to Wolf: "In the wake of the sexual revolution, with the line between 'good' and 'bad' girls always shifting, keeping us unsteady, as it is meant to do, it will not be safe for us to live comfortably in our skins until we say: 'You can no longer separate us out one from another. We are all bad girls.'"

LATINAS IN LOVE SURVEY

Q: Is having sex on the first date a good idea sometimes, always, or never?

A: Seventy-two percent said "Never," and 28 percent said "Sometimes."

A woman is no longer a commodity, but in a modern romance, she's still the prize. Women still want to be pursued, they still want romance, and they still want to be swept away. This lesson does have a worthy underlying message. Put in modern terms, it can be used to remind women to value themselves and understand that most men will take sex any way that they can get it. Many women have tried to separate their heads from their genitals, but it's just not possible for most of us. Try as we might, we just can't "do it" until we're numb. Sexual freedom is a good thing, and if women want to explore it, great. But for Latinas who want a relationship that may lead to something permanent—*tranquilas*. Stop trying to collect those notches on your headboard and get to know the guy first. Make sure you're compatible and that you've established some level of trust, and most importantly, make sure you know what turns you on.

The modern version of this lesson should be: Don't have sex on the first date and remember that good dating is about quality, not quantity.

Choose Your Traditions

LATINA MOMS ARE awesome. We owe them a lot. However, they're not perfect. They sometimes give outdated advice or stunt us with their male-centered hogwash. Still, we have to love our mothers, and mothers have to love their daughters. For better or worse, this cycle of knowledge passing from generation to generation never ends.

A whole new generation of Latina moms is just now starting families. The world their daughters will face holds many new challenges. These new mothers will have to make a choice. They can draw on the cultural traditions their own mothers used to raise them and pass them on to their new daughters. Or they can take a good hard look at those lessons to see which can be used in modern society, which need a little modification, and which ones should be put out with the rest of the garbage.

3

Young Love, First Love

How has falling in love for the first time changed,
and what influences young Latinas today?

Dear Pilar,

My mother is so old-fashioned it drives me crazy! If she had her way, I wouldn't leave the house until I was twenty-one. She won't let me date, so I'm tempted to sneak out, but a little voice inside me says I'd regret it. Still, all my friends have boyfriends. I feel like a freak. How can I get my mom to understand that this is a new millennium?

Catherine, 16

CATHERINE'S LETTER SHOWS the classic generation gap so prevalent between first-generation moms and second-generation daughters. She wants to get out into the dating world badly, yet keeps bumping her head against parental restrictions. *La madre* is worried for good reason—letting daughters loose in this crazy world is a nightmare for parents even if it is a dream for young girls.

We all remember our first date, first kiss, and first love. Young girls will always dream of these milestones. Just wondering who will be the boy who takes them past each romantic benchmark and anticipating when it will all happen dominate conversations and keep teenage girls on the phone, or online, for hours. It's a period in a young girl's life of complete, wide-eyed innocence, where anything's possible, even Prince Charming. It's the stuff about which books are written and daydreams are made.

Once it's lost, however, it's lost forever, and then we wonder, What was the rush? Why was I in such a hurry to get each phase over with and move on to the biggest of the romantic moments for a girl, her first time?

We fondly look back on the very first date and the feeling it gave us of butterflies in the stomach with wingspans that reached our hearts. We cherish the memory of that first meaningful eye contact, the stomach performing triple somersaults, and the first kiss that really did bring on the "vapors" and sweaty palms. As I said in my answer to Catherine, yes, you are correct, *chica,* first love can't be beat, and it's one of the memories that doesn't fade but gets even better with time.

This universal experience remains fairly similar from one generation to the next. Recently, however, there has been a shift away from the social traditions that accompany the first stages of courting so that most romantic benchmarks take place all in one night. The lack of romantic structure has caused some confusion among young women, including young Latinas. And this gives Catherine's mother even more reason for concern.

YOUTHFUL LABELS

GENERATION X—roughly applied to the generation born between 1965 and 1976. This term was popularized by Canadian author Douglas Coupland in his 1991 novel *Generation X: Tales for an Accelerated Culture* and immediately appropriated by the media.

GENERATION Y—applied to those born directly after Gen Xers in the years 1977 to 1987, is a sociological extension of Generation X and generally means someone who grew up in the decade after Generation X.

GENERATION Ñ—applies to Latino Gen Xers (hence the tilde). This term was coined by publisher Bill Teck in the Miami-based magazine *Generation Ñ* and is used widely in Latino media.

Today's teenagers to thirty-somethings are generally referred to as Generations X, Y, and Ñ. Lumping young people under these designations seems unfair, even malicious, because it strips them of character and individuality, proving that they are neither understood nor appreciated by older generations. Stamped with a generic sociological brand, the younger generation, Latinas included, feels it has been labeled and shelved by everyone over forty, including their parents. Young women often mistrust their mothers and rely more on their peers, who seem to really understand them. Television plays a stronger role in defining their values and shaping their morality. The children of divorced or workaholic parents, they have little faith in marriage (yet seem to have a great respect for the institution) and a deep resentment for parents who left them alone or ignored them because of their drive to make money. "Acting out" takes on a whole new dimension, from unwanted pregnancies to drug use. Everything old, it seems, is bad, and everything new is good.

Columnist Jeff Miller expresses his frustration in a 2002 column written for *University Wire*: "Congratulations, students! If you didn't know it already, you're officially members of Generation Y. Until recently, I thought we were all late-blooming Generation Xers, but evidently, the people who decide to make these classifications felt it was time for a new group to be named, recognized, and lumped together. I don't know about the rest of you, but I think this is terrific. Finally we've broken free of the mocha drinking, anti-nuptial, and generally apathetic-toward-everything stereotype that our immediate predecessors did such a wonderful job of getting themselves railed into. Now is the time for Generation Y. But what a weak title for as important a sociological stereotype as we are . . . come on—Generation Y? What does that mean? Is that all we are—just the next barely recognizable group after Generation X?"

Clearly, these unflattering categories do little to ingratiate adults to kids, especially when compared to the term used to describe their parents. Generations X, Y, and Ñ are the children of Baby Boomers, a whole generation of adults who were born from the 1940s through the 1960s—significant historical decades in the nation's history. The term

"Baby Boomers" reflects the great expectations of this post–World War II generation. It's catchy, descriptive, and accurately describes another perk of the period—heightened sexual activity during this postwar prosperity that resulted in a baby boom. According to a 1997 article by Bob Losyk in *The Futurist*, the baby boom took place between 1946 and 1964, when the birth rate peaked at 25.3 births per thousand people.

The following eleven years when the Gen Xers were born, 1965–1976, are considered a "baby bust" period because the birth rate fell to 14.6 births per thousand. The term "Generation X" reflects this not-so-fertile period and seems more like a brush-off by sociologists and demographers than an attempt at understanding. Indeed, the happy-go-lucky boomers have had difficulty understanding their precocious, serious, and conservative offspring. Baby Boomers are people whose parents were dealing with their own Depression Era angst and wanted to ensure that their children would never face a similar hardship. Consequently, Boomers were generally well provided for, especially financially, and represent one of the best-educated sectors of society. They were encouraged to "reach for the stars" and "follow their dreams," in other words, to be successful and make money.

Fashions today clearly reflect a nostalgia for the sixties and seventies, decades of experimentation and cultural growth. Besides sex, drugs, and rock 'n' roll, there was also the Vietnam War, the Civil Rights and women's movements, the Space Race, and the Beatles. The world survived all these revolutionary changes.

In contrast, what influences did the next generation grow up with? The 1980s were a cultural black hole that focused on how much money one could acquire, regardless of the impact. There were some exciting backlashes, like punk music, but besides *Dallas* and *Dynasty* reruns, the entire eighties has little to show for itself. Generation X experienced new wave music, the Challenger explosion, homelessness, and Reagan Era deregulation that drastically cut social programs, like college loans and grants, which limited access to a higher education. This was followed by the Bush era of illicit wars fought for "national interest" (read: Oil) and the band that could have been the next Beatles: Nirvana. The band's brilliant but dysfunctional leader, Kurt Cobain took his life and although the band spawned grunge music, the genre lacked direction and inspiration without the gifted Cobain.

It is natural, perhaps, for the younger generation to feel let down by the adults who shaped their formative years. They mistrust and feel patronized by advertisers and media moguls. This generation respects honesty and does not appreciate advertising that seemingly panders to them. For Generations X, Y, and Ñ, the added attention is not the kind they want. They intuit that advertising and corporate executives see them as an exploitable second gold rush and nothing more.

What do demographers really know about this age group? Many predict that this generation has a bright future based on their multi-ethnicity, computer literacy, and sophistication. But being saddled with a letter X, Y, or Ñ implies that this is a generation with an identity crisis. They are a mass of contradictions: Portrayed as rebels, they are much more conservative than their music or fashion would suggest. They mistrust the motives of adults yet have a steadfast appreciation for honesty (any traces of a secret agenda are quickly and completely condemned). Perhaps years of patronization and pandering have made them thirst for a straightforward, no-nonsense approach. At the same time, they're trendy and veritable slaves to fashion. They appreciate, follow, and set fads fairly regularly. They love old things but dis the people who invented them (mainly Baby Boomers). They want to be respected but are not ready to commit to anything. They were raised by parents who adopted a kinder, gentler approach to parenting, and yet they're angry. Even with all these contradictions, this generation feels it has something to say and responds well when treated fairly and with respect.

MTV's get-out-the-vote effort, Rock the Vote, took off with the 1992 presidential campaign and helped mobilize eighteen-to-twenty-somethings to participate in the democratic process. The younger generation contributed significantly to Bill Clinton's election to the presidency. When Clinton appeared on MTV, he looked cool and relaxed and answered questions thoughtfully and in earnest. His opponent, incumbent President George Bush, was clearly uncomfortable, incredibly unhip, and a little afraid when it was his turn to appear on MTV. Seven years later, when the Clinton sex scandal emerged, this group, in on-the-street interviews and televised town hall meetings, vented their disgust. It wasn't the sex that bothered them; it was Clinton's ability to tell a bald-faced lie on national television. Their disappointment was evident at the polls in 2000, when they stayed home.

In general, when Baby Boomers were young, they were hopeful and positive about their futures. Their children, however, are cynical and jaded. Since they have little confidence in their future, they live life much more in the moment. This may explain the increased drug use by the younger generations and heightened sexual activity.

Are they as confused as we like to think they are? Are the tags X,

Y, or Ñ a bit unfair? Aren't the problems of youth still the problems of youth? The answer across the board is yes. The dilemmas of this generation are similar to those of former generations at the same age. We've all mistrusted our parents at one time or another and had a gut-level aversion to authority figures. We've all struggled with who we are, how we're perceived, and what we want to be when we grow up. Young people today suffer the same afflictions, but what's different are the coping mechanisms available to young people and the social mores that act as guidelines when a parent's advice is unacceptable. Also, this generation, perhaps because its outlook on the future is bleak, is in a bit of a rush. They seem anxious to get life's benchmarks out of the way. In their rush to adulthood, however, many seem to forget how a baby is made. The clearest indication of this is the rise in the teen pregnancy rate over the past few years, and the fact that Latinas experience a significantly higher pregnancy rate.

TEENAGE PREGNANCY

Ten percent of all girls ages fifteen through nineteen become mothers. The pregnancy rate for Latinas (148.7 per thousand in this age group) is more than twice that for non-Hispanic whites (65.1 per thousand) and slightly lower than that of non-Hispanic black girls (170.4 per thousand).

Source: 2000 U.S. Census

Tradition is particularly despised by this generation, so some good traditions, like dating, have been rejected. Rather than going out in pairs, young people interact socially in coed groups. The danger here is that the group's rules can overpower individual decisions. Peer pressure is difficult enough in school, but formerly, at the end of the day, kids could escape it and return home for reassurance and advice. If a group environment is maintained after school in a social setting, the sexual tension between boys and girls can escalate. Parents too are deceived that the group environment is a safer situation, especially for their daughters, when in fact, outside of the group and on a date, a boy and girl may be more likely to listen to their own inner voices. Outside of the group, both the boy and girl have only to deal with each other, and acceptance or rejection can happen privately. These decisions are much more difficult to make in front of the group where the tendency is to go along. The consequences, especially for girls, can be devastating.

In "The Lost Children of Rockdale Country," a 2000 *Frontline* documentary about a syphilis outbreak in suburban Atlanta, thirteen- and fourteen-year-old girls spoke about their first sexual experiences. Bored with life in suburbia, they admitted that having sex was just something new to do. They hung out with a group of about ten boys and girls. They were filmed outside of bowling allies or in the parking lot of a strip mall smoking, drinking, and making out. The girls were loud and obnoxious in the group, but when interviewed at home, they were much more thoughtful and contrite. They admitted that losing their virginity seemed to happen on impulse, under the influence of alcohol, and encouraged by the group. Many of their friends had done it, so the girls decided to try it. The consensus was that they regretted having made that sexual decision at such a young age and with so little consideration about the consequences. One girl even decided to reclaim her virginity and had taken a vow of chastity for her remaining years in high school.

The issue wasn't addressed in the documentary, but I think dating could have helped these girls. These kids were in a rush to grow up, and they made the kinds of mistakes that some adults do, including having unprotected sex, and the outcome was revealed en masse.

LATINAS IN LOVE SURVEY

Q: What's the best age for women and men to lose their virginity?

A: Sixty percent felt that ages eighteen to twenty-one was the ideal range for both sexes.

For this generation, the concept of dating seems arcane, rigid, and pointless. In truth, dating has changed and evolved over time. "Girls are much more forward than they used to be," commented one insightful Generation Ñ Latina. "They'll call boys or even pick them up for a date. One friend did this and the boy asked her, 'Why are you doing this? Why are you going out with a guy like me when I don't even have a car?' After that, he started taking her for granted. I think it went to his head."

Indeed, this generation is much more forward, in many ways. According to a 1999 article in *MIN's New Media Report*, the sexual content on Generation X and Y chat rooms and the Web sites they frequent are fairly sexually explicit. According to the article, "The Generation X and Y segments that favor these sites seem eager to finish the Sexual Revolution that older, Viagra-popping boomers started. Not only do many editors find that teens and twenty-somethings feel more open and even entitled to a good sex life, but older gender boundaries are melting quickly." The ratio of male to female readers (normally sixty to forty) at one site evens out among eighteen to twenty-five year olds, reflecting openness among young women toward franker sexual material, the article adds.

The young modern Latina is not immune to the tendencies of her generation. Like her friends, she will question authority and struggle for respect. Many share the same attitude toward dating as their peers and find the concept ridiculous. They also make the same mistake as girls in the mainstream population and rush to have sex before getting to know the guy.

On top of feeling the pressures of Generation Y, there is the long-standing Latino tradition of not discussing sex. Modern Latino parents struggle with acknowledging their children as sexual beings, and many times postpone the discussion until it's too late. In her book, Dr. Ana Nogales notes, "Every day in the United States, 302 Latino babies are born to Latino mothers. And yet, parents often think that the way to prevent teenage pregnancy is to not talk about it."

RESOURCES FOR YOUNG LATINAS

Here are some Latino organizations that you might find useful. They specialize in dealing with birth control issues, fighting teen pregnancy, and fostering self-esteem in girls.

- The ASPIRA Association, 1444 Eye Street, NW, Suite 800, Washington, DC 20005; 202-835-3600
- National Alliance of Hispanic Health, 1501 16th Street, NW, Washington, DC 20036; 202-387-5000
- Puerto Rican Development and Youth Resource Center Inc., 997 N. Clinton Avenue, Rochester, NY 14621; 585-325-3570
- National Latina Health Network, 1680 Wisconsin Ave., NW, #2, Washington, DC 20007; 202-965-9633
- Hispanic Magazine Online—The Web site for *Hispanic* with tools for teens including an advice column. www.hispaniconline.com
- Blue Jean online—The Web site for *Blue Jean* magazine, one of the oldest publications targeting young women with a positive message as well as fashion. www.bluejeanonline.com
- www.hispanicoutlook.com—The Web site for *The Hispanic Outlook on Higher Education* offers information to teens about college including scholarships and financial aid.
- www.teenpregnancy.org—Official Web site for the National Campaign to Stop Teen Pregnancy

As a columnist, I have received letters from young teenage Latinas who have been swept away by Internet encounters. Again, the more things change, the more they stay the same. In the 1970s it was the citizens band (CB) radio. In the new millennium, it's the Internet. Apparently, people still like to talk to and flirt with mysterious strangers. With a CB, you judged someone's attractiveness by his or her voice. On the Internet, all you're seeing are typed words, which can be more provocative.

As a teenager, I remember cruising around town for hours with my sister and a friend who had a CB and talking to some guys. It was all fun and exciting until we decided to meet in a grocery store parking lot. One look at them, and we said, "Never mind." On the Internet, so much of the person on the other keyboard is manufactured into a fantasy that it can be dangerous, especially for younger people. One young Latina wrote me in earnest about a boy she claimed to love, desperately, but who lived in another state. He had suggested that she move across the country and join him, because he was desperate to be with her. They had had a tiff, however, over who loved whom more. Sensing some mistrust toward him, she entered a chat room that she and her "boyfriend" frequented, but used a false name. Her boyfriend was there, so she began flirting with him. Almost immediately, he flirted back. Heartbroken, she wrote me for advice. It astounded her that he could flirt with another girl right after chatting with her. I told her not to get carried away with an Internet romance and that the only way to have a real relationship was to see someone in person and get to know him over time. She wrote back that she had taken my advice and broken up with him. Whew!

MOTHER KNOWS BEST

The National Longitudinal Study of Adolescent Health (Add Health), a federally funded survey conducted by the University of Carolina at Chapel Hill, revealed that mothers who have established a good relationship with their children, especially their daughters, should feel free to offer advice because their children are more likely to take it. "When teens perceive that their mothers oppose their having sex, they are less likely to do so," the study reported. Add Health data was studied by the *Journal of Adolescent Health* and *Archives of Pediatric and Adolescent Medicine* and each published the results in September of 2002.

To ask this generation to do some old-fashioned "courting" may be asking the impossible, but with their love of nostalgia and their confusion about how to reconcile the tenets of the women's movement with the rules of romance, they might just embrace this concept. To begin with, the practice is much more flexible today than in the past. It used to be that a young woman would never be allowed to be alone with a boy. Dating consisted of socializing at home or in public with chaperones, usually parents or older siblings. Today that would probably never happen. Instead of chaperones, parents use curfews or provide the transportation to and from the date as a means of supervising what goes on. The formality is gone, but the intention is still the same.

What used to consist of sitting in the parlor and exchanging a few words has evolved into going to the movies and grabbing something to eat. The date doesn't have to be extravagant, certainly not in high school, but the intention is still the same—to get to know each other. It may sound incredibly unromantic, but the main objective is to talk and listen and then decide if you want to make the additional investment of time to get to know your date better. Those of us who have actually been on a date can testify that they can be very romantic, even with this practical objective tucked away at the back of your mind.

Before allowing dating, however, parents need to prepare their children on some of the basic rules regarding sex. Parents have long been encouraged to talk about sex with their children, but many still rely on teachers to tackle the subject. Latina moms especially, who tend to be more reserved when it comes to talking about sex, need to fight this temptation. Educational films about puberty and sex will give kids the biological information they need, but they do not encourage kids that a date is a fun thing. As an addendum to sex education, kids should also receive tips on dating, the dos and don'ts, the whys and hows. Many parents would rather believe that their children are still babies, but denial will only cause kids to venture out on their own. They don't want to believe that their children, especially daughters, are becoming sexual, so they take a passive rather than an active approach to the situation. One friend told me that once her daughter became a senior in high school, and started dating, she got the feeling that sex was on her mind. She discussed it with her daughter but then added that she forbade her to have sex until she was in college. Remarkably, her daughter seemed relieved. "I made the decision for her so she didn't have to worry any more," she said.

Discussing sex is never easy for parents. My mother never addressed
the subject. Luckily my older sister had received those pamphlets that
mothers passed to daughters about becoming a woman. Written in the
1950s, however, they usually added to the confusion instead of clari-
fying it. My sister shared them with me, but I was more concerned
with my menstrual cycle than about the sex act. When my mother
asked me if I had any questions, months after my first period, I told
her that Lisa (my sister) had passed the pamphlets on to me. The
youngest of three girls, I learned about sex from talking to my sisters
mainly, and to my friends secondarily. I even remember the moment
that I realized that a boy's "wee-wee" had to penetrate a girl's "woo-
woo" to make a baby. I was in our front yard, for some reason, and our
next-door neighbor was visiting with my sisters and me. We must have
been talking about boys or sex because suddenly, I had a moment of
clarity. I turned to our neighbor, who was a few years older than my
oldest sister, probably seventeen or so, and looked at her and asked, "Is
that really how it happens?" "Yes," she responded, to which I cried,

"Eeeuuw, gross!" Incredibly, her response was, "I think it's beautiful."
As a twelve-year-old, however, I was devastated.

Parents can't shy away from talking to children about sex and dating, especially once puberty sets in. If today's girls could understand
the responsibilities and consequences that come from sex, besides the
pure enjoyment, they may not be so quick to dive in. Then as a segue,
parents can move on to the next stage of the conversation and talk
about one of the most important tools for coping with this new
responsibility—dating.

LATINAS IN LOVE SURVEY

Q: How would you describe the perfect date?

A: Most respondents said getting to know each other
was essential. One Latina responded: "An ideal date
is dinner and skipping the movie because the conversation is too good."

I didn't quite learn about sex on the street, but almost. Luckily, I had
older sisters, and my mother had the presence of mind to send us to a
Catholic, all-girls high school. Dating, for me, really took off in college
since in high school my only interaction with boys came after school
when several, usually from the boys' high school located nearby, would
cruise around the parking lot, flirting and chatting. Every Friday night
there was a high school dance hosted alternatively by the local Catholic

high schools. Inevitably the DJ would announce a Sadie Hawkins dance or "lady's choice," and girls got to ask the boys to dance. Additionally, there were junior and senior proms and semiformal dances at each school. At the all-girl schools, Ursuline, Providence, and Incarnate Word, the girls got to ask the boys out.

I went to both of mine and was asked by a couple of boys to theirs. I was set up by my friends the first year (that never works) and took the boy of my dreams to the semiformal and a different boy of my dreams to the prom the next year. Both nights were glorious, although my lack of experience did lead me to bungle my date's attempted kiss (and my first) at the end of the prom. He took it personally, and that was the end of that. I did get kissed later that year, and although my prom date was a witness, it was not by him, unfortunately. Like those young girls in Georgia, I just wanted to get it over with, but in my case it was kissing, not intercourse. That kind of naiveté is completely appropriate in high school, but unfortunately, it's much less common today.

Both boys and girls are uncomfortable about the process and what they should or should not do on a date. The rules used to be so clear. Girls did nothing but sit around and wait to be asked out, and on the date the boys were expected to impress them, not the other way around. Girls today don't feel that a boy should have to pay (nor do the boys), boys don't know how to ask a girl out, and both don't understand the purpose of it all. For this generation, dating is a useless, somewhat deceptive exercise. The concept of being on your best behavior, getting dressed up, and trying to impress each other has an artificial quality that the younger generation rejects. They have it all wrong, of course, and this is where parents must get involved.

THE ABCs OF DATING

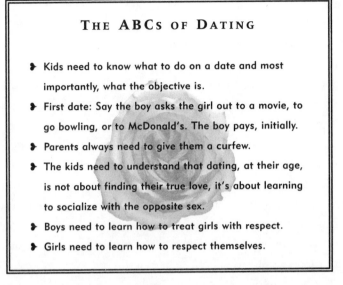

- ❧ Kids need to know what to do on a date and most importantly, what the objective is.
- ❧ First date: Say the boy asks the girl out to a movie, to go bowling, or to McDonald's. The boy pays, initially.
- ❧ Parents always need to give them a curfew.
- ❧ The kids need to understand that dating, at their age, is not about finding their true love, it's about learning to socialize with the opposite sex.
- ❧ Boys need to learn how to treat girls with respect.
- ❧ Girls need to learn how to respect themselves.

In nature, from ants to humans, the female is usually the prize and it's a fact of nature, not an outmoded custom that females tend to be choosey because of their roles as mothers. In the dating game, many young women have lost sight of their innate value. Dating can help remind them that they are the prize, and it's not ridiculous to think of themselves that way. Parents should coach their daughters properly and although they may be embarrassed at first, they'll soon learn that the boys who give them the most grief about opening doors or paying for dinner will definitely fall short as boyfriends, husbands, or fathers.

Older Latinas know that there is a point to dating. Basically, it helps men and women avoid wasting their time on a bad relationship. You can find out in one night whether you want to see this person ever again. This is when a couple gets to know each other and, if all goes well, lays the foundation for a future relationship. On the other hand, it's also when they find out whether or not there's any need to move forward. Dating gives clues to compatibility but in order for it to work, women must have a very clear idea of what they want. They need to know what kind of behavior they will accept and what they will not. Most importantly, they need to believe that they are the prize, that they are desirable, and that they're worth pursuing. This does not mean that a man shouldn't have the same clear ideas of what he wants, but to say so would be redundant—guys generally know what they want. For women, and especially for Latinas, our need to nurture and please puts us in a muddle, and we can forget about ourselves in the process. Once we lose sight of what we want, we embark on a slippery slope toward a bad relationship.

In matters of the heart, it's very hard to be logical, but girls need to try to maintain some type of objectivity when dating. For instance, a young Latina should not approach each date as if he is the next Mr. Right. She needs to tell herself he's just a person she finds attractive and who she would like to get to know better. It's also important to learn from each date. On the first few dates, a girl may find it hard to identify specific behavior that she won't accept, but as she moves on, that list will inevitably take shape and begin to grow. This is also a good time to develop an ear for the little voice inside you. It's never wrong, and it will raise a red flag on a date when a boy exhibits unacceptable behavior, such as not opening doors, walking ten paces ahead of you, or dominating the conversation. The behavior I hated most was when a guy didn't call the next day after a date and left me wondering as to whether or not it had gone well. I felt so manipulated. The first thing the man who is now my husband did after our first date was to call me—and the rest is history! Your little voice is the best defense against a bad relationship. Trust yourself.

There is another safeguard, but it's been out of vogue for decades. That special, quaint safeguard is virginity.

LATINAS IN LOVE SURVEY

Q: How would you describe the worst kind of date?

A: Thoughtlessness and a big ego are spoilers. One Latina responded: "He's late or flakes. He doesn't have a plan as to where to take you. He asks where you want to go, then complains about the music or food or doesn't eat at all. Can't keep up a conversation. Drops you off at the curb."

Without dating, this younger generation, just as curious as any other teenagers, may proceed straight to having sex, which is unfortunate for both boys and girls. Like the children in the *Frontline* documentary, young Latinas are also vulnerable to peer pressure, boredom, and low self-esteem, the latter being the most dangerous. To give up her virginity just because her friends have is an unfortunate choice and one that can never be erased. Honestly, girls, your virginity is not a thorn in your libido that needs to be plucked. It's a safeguard against having a bad first sexual experience that you can never quite forget. By holding out, girls can really weed out a lot of losers, and although I don't believe all men are dogs, the ones who drop you if you don't put out definitely fall into that category. But low-self esteem can cause a young Latina to be convinced that having sex will "prove" her love and consequently, she'll get love in return.

The fact is, sex at this age is rarely about love and more about curiosity. A teenager's hormones are racing and those first moments of boy-craziness can be sublime. I know teenagers will hate me for this, but love really is a mature emotion. Nothing may ever feel as exhilarating as young love, first love, but it's also called puppy love for a good reason. Looking back, I thought my heart would break and my world would end over one boy after another. I cried rivers of tears and truly believed that no one would ever mean as much as the boy *du jour*. I don't mean to sound unromantic, but you do get over it. Broken hearts do mend. Woody Allen put it beautifully in *Hannah and Her Sisters* when, after marrying his ex-wife's sister, his character remarked, "The heart is a very, very resilient little muscle."

LATINAS IN LOVE SURVEY

Q: Is having sex on the first date a good idea—always, usually, sometimes, or never?

A: Seventy-two percent said "never," and 28 percent said "sometimes."

Having sex before developing any kind of relationship means youngsters will learn to build a relationship from the top down rather than from the bottom up. What comes after the intimate experience? No matter how hard we try or how many lovers we have, women are rarely completely numb to sex. A recent study found that women produce the same hormone when having sex as they do when breast-feeding; in other words, we bond with our sex partner. For women, sex is a romanticized gift to be saved for the right person. When it's thrown away, girls may lose their sexual perspective and, consequently, their equilibrium when it comes to relationships. They'll want to start a relationship with sex because it gives them a feeling of being loved, but the morning after, they'll have little objectivity when they see unacceptable behavior. It's much harder to accept that a guy's not "all that" after having sex with him than, say, if you had just gone to a movie or Starbucks for coffee.

Younger Latinas like Catherine are still raised with their mothers' provincial attitudes, but second- or third-generation Latinas have also been influenced by popular American culture, and in a good way. Young women in their twenties and thirties carry a confidence that their mothers didn't have. The previous generation may have broken barriers, but these women are not going to spend their time saying thank you. They're going forward into careers with the potential of being promoted beyond the glass ceiling that their mothers faced early in their careers. As professionals, this generation is confident, and that should translate into healthy relationships, provided they get back to dating and practicing a little restraint when it comes to sex. I love the show *Sex and the City*, but I watch it as a married woman. I wonder if single Latinas think it's so great. I like the girl talk, but when one character contracted chlamydia and had to make of list of all the men she'd slept with in order to find the culprit, and the list included more than thirty names, I was appalled.

Latinas young and old don't need to be modeling the loose behavior portrayed in shows like *Sex and the City*—the shoes, however, are fabulous. I'm not suggesting women should be virgins when they get married, but I am saying, take your time! Get to know the boy, but most importantly, get to know yourself.

Luscious Latinas

Can a stereotype be a good thing?

Querida Amiga Mía,

I've always been proud to be a Latina. I know that some men, especially non-Latinos, may get the wrong idea about me because I'm Latina, but I still like being considered exotic and sexy. I applaud Jennifer Lopez and Salma Hayek for being so beautiful and the epitome of a Latina. It sounds bad, but I like to think that every man who's not with a Latina has one tucked away in his fantasies. My attitude does make it hard for me to get along with white women. Is it my problem or theirs?

Letitia, 30

*L*ETITIA HAS HIT upon a truism. It's great to be a Latina, and we know it. We're blessed with great genes, good values, and a culture that is as rich as it is old. When it comes to the dating game, however, we're also frequently blessed with features and an attitude that lead some to refer to us as "luscious." When I answered Letitia, I didn't want to dampen her enthusiasm, so I said her confidence was commendable but that sometimes an outward show of confidence can evoke envy from others. But in the dating world, that self-assurance will come in handy.

The word "luscious" leans toward being complimentary because lusciousness infers desirability. But in reality, to be a called a luscious Latina is a backhanded compliment. Luscious is a tongueful. It says a woman is sexy, curvy, fleshy, voluptuous, and sought after—so far, no problem. To be luscious is to be an object of desire, and while the word "desire" is great, the word "object" is a big problem. It implies that women are nonentities, just a collection of eyes, lips, arms, legs, tits, and ass. We really don't mind if men appreciate our attributes as long as they include our brain as one of them. If there's something all women hate, it's being objectified.

But desire is quite different, and this is where both sexes tend to get in a muddle. When it comes to desire, most women need it, want it, look for it, dress for it, and fantasize about it, yet we also feel guilty about it. This is not the image of the modern woman who emerged from the sixties and the women's movement. Today's woman is supposed to gain confidence from her own accomplishments and talent and certainly not define herself by how attractive men find her. Well, that philosophy works well at the office, but it's much harder to apply in the bedroom. We don't just want equality in our paychecks—we also want equality in our orgasms!

To be truly equal in the bedroom requires a certain amount of chemistry, attraction, and lust, and Latinas are well versed on the art of seduction. They know that cotton briefs just don't compare to black stockings and a garter belt, and that they're just as effective on the woman who's wearing them as the man who's unsnapping them. *Somos muy coquetas.* We're natural flirts, so to be called a "luscious Latina" may not be our ultimate goal, but it's also not a term we're completely ready to abandon.

The problems associated with the term are subtle and difficult to explain. We know this stereotype is bad for us, but we're not willing to give it up. It's similar to the double-edged sword people of color face when it comes to vice advertising. We know that people of color, especially in poor neighborhoods, are targeted by the tobacco and liquor industries through advertising on billboards, radio, and in community newspapers. Many groups have successfully protested against that kind of promotion in their neighborhoods. However, when it comes to advertising in minority publications, liquor and tobacco are the first, and sometimes the only ones, to buy ad space. Consequently, they contribute to that publication's success and that does have a trickle-down effect on communities of color in the form of jobs, economic stability, and minority entrepreneurship. Critics say that those publications should refuse to accept these ads, but when more appealing advertisers refuse to meet with their ad reps, is it really fair to hold small businesses up to such a standard? How is this similar to the Luscious Latina moniker? It may be bad for us but we're not willing to give it up because there is a benefit attached. The lusciousness will grab a man's attention but once we've got it, we want him to get to know the real Latina inside.

HOLLYWOOD'S CHANGING IMAGE OF THE LUSCIOUS LATINA

❥ 1920s—Delores del Río

❥ 1930s—Lupe Vélez

❥ 1940s—Rita Hayworth, Carmen Miranda

❥ 1950s—Linda Cristal

❥ 1960s—Rita Moreno

❥ 1970s—Raquel Welch

❥ 1980s—Sonia Braga

❥ 1990s and beyond—Salma Hayek, Jennifer Lopez

The Luscious Stereotype

THE HISTORY OF the luscious Latina stereotype can be traced back to Hollywood, which portrayed Latinas early on as spitfires. This image promoted the stereotype of Latinas as high-strung, volatile, aggressive, and even dangerous. At the other end of the spectrum, Hollywood also cast Latinas as maids, promoting stereotypical views of them as meek and subservient. There is no better medium for typecasting than movies.

Dolores del Río (Dolores Martínez Ansúnsolo López Negrete) initially broke the color barrier for Latinas in Hollywood during the twenties. Because she fit the mold of an "exotic," the Mexican actress was cast in trendy films set in the South Pacific. Following on her heels was the first Latina spitfire, Lupe Vélez (Guadalupe Villalobos Vélez). Considered a B-movie actress, Vélez created a comedic role by speaking with a heavy accent and resorting to rapid-fire Spanish when annoyed. This spitfire image—an oversexed and overly emotional woman—was unflattering.

In the thirties and forties, Rita Hayworth (Margarita Cansino) grew in popularity but only after she received a Hollywood transformation. The originally dark-haired Hayworth played the dark lady and was most noted for a bar room dance to "La Cucaracha" in the film *Hit the Saddle* (1937). In *The Hispanic American Almanac*, writer Nicolás Kanellos explains that it wasn't until Hayworth married businessman Edward Judson, "who helped her see that being a Hispanic limited her work to a cinematic loose woman," that she changed her image. Hayworth transformed herself from the dark lady to an auburn-haired love goddess.

Over time, images on the big screen impacted social perceptions. Latinas began to experience treatment in their jobs and at the grocery store that reflected these stereotypes. The Civil Rights movement and the women's movement helped to mobilize Latinos to demand changes and end the harmful stereotypes. In the seventies, Latinos mobilized the Chicano Movement, which focused on education, employment, and political empowerment. Latinas were at the forefront of this movement; for example, Dolores Huerta co-founded the United Farm Workers with Cesar Chavez and worked by his side until his death in 1993.

Over the decades, Latinas like Hayworth and Raquel Welch have been elevated to sex symbol status. The popularity of these actresses, however, did not come without a price. Many times they were type-cast into playing just one kind of woman and for some, like Welch (Jo Raquel Tejada), the fact that she was a Latina was not revealed until much later in her career.

Young Latinas will always need role models. Rita Moreno (Rosita Dolores Alverio) suffered the same setbacks as her predecessors and con-temporaries, but she took on the position of role model. Her excep-tional career began in the fifties when she was cast in the Broadway and film versions of *The King and I*. Her breakthrough role, of course, was as Anita in *Westside Story*. Unfortunately, the Academy Award she won for her portrayal did not improve her clout; it only brought her more of the same roles. She chose to walk away from the business until Hollywood producers and directors realized that Latinos as actors had much more to offer than their sensuality. Eventually she put together a body of work that is as diverse as it is brilliant. She did not trade in her sex appeal; she just made Tinsel Town recognize her talent and intelli-gence. Moreno is also one of the few performers of any ethnic group who has won an Oscar, a Tony, a Grammy, and an Emmy.

Over the years, Latinas in Hollywood have struggled due to the lack of adequate roles for them to play. Each decade can boast a few break-out exceptions, like del Rio in the 1930s or Moreno in the 1960s, but generally, the industry has not welcomed Latinas. In the nineties, how-ever, several names emerged. Actresses like Salma Hayek, Jennifer Lopez, and Cameron Diaz were not only successful in Hollywood, they also parlayed their talent into creating their own production companies and increasing their creative clout. They have converted their success into power, and that translates into better roles. Although they can still play the provocative female, they can also choose to play historical figures, spies, geeks, cops, teachers, or wedding planners. Hayek and Lopez continue to promote an image of Latinas as exotic and desirable, but due to the double-edged nature of the luscious Latina image, both actresses have chosen their film projects carefully. Director Robert Rodriguez introduced Hayek to American audiences in his 1997 film *Desperado*. Although she received credit for a smart performance in a straight role (her character just happened to be Latino and luscious), her breakthrough performances followed *Desperado*. Indeed, Hayek has practically reintroduced the spitfire and the dark lady. In the Rodriguez film, *From Dusk Till Dawn*, Hayek makes a cameo appearance in a seductive dance number in which she wears a bikini, a headdress, and an Albino boa constrictor. The beautiful Mexican actress created a stunningly provocative moment in the film with barely a line of dialogue. In her next project, *Fools Rush In*, she was paired with Matthew Perry in a romantic comedy. The film explores the culture clash between Latinos and whites, but Hayek is clearly the spitfire to Perry's cardboard Anglo male. She took a satiric stab at the spitfire by playing a heavenly muse in *Dogma*, where her character is one of the Universe's higher beings that masquerades as a stripper on Earth. Her most ambitious project yet, Frida, a biopic on the life of Mexican artist Frida Kahlo, is clearly a substantial coup for Hayek. Still considered a rare event, in this film a Mexican actress actually portrays a famous Mexican historical figure.

Even today, Latinas rarely get to play Latinas. Mainstream directors hardly seem to consider the possibility. For example, in the Academy Award–winning film *A Beautiful Mind*, Jennifer Connelly played Alicia Nash, the wife of mathematical genius John Nash and won an

Academy Award for her performance. What was overlooked was that Alicia Nash was very definitely a Latina; a native of El Salvador, in fact. After director Ron Howard received his Academy Awards for best director and best picture, he was asked by a wonderfully bold Latino reporter about why Mrs. Nash's ethnicity was ignored in the movie. Howard responded, "There were so many other nuances to this character that we wanted to explore." *¡Pinche* Opie!

Lisa Navarette, deputy vice president of the National Council of La Raza, sums up the problem behind this lack of understanding in Hollywood in a 2002 column in *Hispanic Link Weekly Report*. "In an industry which controls the most powerful media in the world, the stereotyping of Latinos in films has kept our community invisible and powerless . . . this is what makes Alicia Nash's whitewashing so depressing. We could have witnessed the portrayal of a true rarity, a three-dimensional Latina role model, by a well known, critically acclaimed actress. Even better, they could have provided a career-making opportunity to a Latina actress. But most of all, this acclaimed movie could have shown the millions who have seen it that this brilliant, accomplished woman . . . was also a Salvadoran immigrant."

Clearly affected by the view of Latinos in Hollywood, Hayek has been the most outspoken of her contemporaries. When asked about the *Frida* project and why she chose to make the movie, she responded, "I'm not willing to wait for Hollywood to create Latino characters for me to play. I decided to create them myself." Other actresses who hadn't publicly acknowledged their Latina-ness are now embracing it. After critically acclaimed performances in the film *Tortilla Soup* (2001) and the television series *American Family* (2002), Raquel Welch hit the talk show circuit to promote both projects. When asked about the Latino nature of each role, she happily informed the audience that her father was Bolivian and that it's not such a stretch after all to be cast as the eccentric *tía* (in *American Family*) or overly optimistic husband hunter (in *Tortilla Soup*). Many Latinos who already knew the truth cheered Welch, and younger Latinas, who perhaps weren't aware of her real ethnicity, found a new luscious Latina to emulate.

Jennifer Lopez promotes the Latina image more as a celebrity and in her music videos than in her film roles. Her breakthrough came in 1996 when she starred in *Selena* in the title role. Since then, she's played an FBI agent, a scientist, and a wedding planner, to name a few, in films that cover all the genres, from science fiction to romantic comedy. Her body of work has captured her charm and demonstrated her range as an actress but has done little to promote the luscious Latina stereotype. In fact, you could argue she turns the stereotype on its head by going after non-Latino roles, therefore opening up more options for Latino actors.

The off-screen J. Lo is quite another story. Videos for her CDs *On the Six* (2000) and *J. Lo* (2001) capitalize on her dancing ability and sultriness—she even strips down to her underwear. She appears to appreciate a headline, and her love life has become a media event. Her love life has been impetuous but sincere, and she has said, "I'm stupid when I fall in love." Although she married her first husband only months after meeting him and divorced him in just over a year, then married her second husband seemingly on the rebound from her failed three-year relationship with Sean "Puffy" Combs, and then divorced him in less then a year, she seems to be in earnest about the man she loves. Her fashion sense also grabs attention. On most occasions, she looks exquisite, but she loves going to the extreme—remember the transparent but elegant Gucci dress and mink-hair eyelashes she wore for the 2001 Academy Awards? But she wore the outfit that topped them all to the 2000 Grammy Awards. She's still remembered for that sheer, full-length, lime green print Versace shirtdress, unbuttoned to her navel. This girlfriend is clearly all about being luscious.

HOLLYWOOD ACTIVISTS

Here are some organizations you can contact if you want your voice to be heard in Hollywood:

- ALMA Awards, sponsored by National Council of La Raza (NCLR), 1111 Nineteenth St., NW, Suite 1000, Washington, DC 20036; 202-785-5384
- Nosotros (one of the oldest Latino actor advocacy groups), 650 N. Bronson Avenue, #102, Hollywood, CA 90004; 323-465-4167
- Hispanic Organization of Latin Actors (HOLA), 250 W. 65th St., New York, NY 10023-6403; 212-665-6237
- *Latin Heat* trade magazine for Latinos in Hollywood, P.O. Box 27, West Covina, CA 91793; 626-917-2160
- www.premiereweekend.org—The Web site of the Premier Weekend Club, an organization promoting support of Latino films, lists opening dates for upcoming Latino films and other information about Latinos in Hollywood.

Like the Latina actresses before them, Hayek, Lopez, Diaz, Penelope Cruz, Elizabeth Peña, Constance Marie, and a slew of others have pushed Hollywood to expand its view of Latinas to real, three-dimensional characters. Some are still spitfires and a few are still maids, but more and more these characters are doctors, lawyers, or police-women as well as wives, mothers, sisters, lovers, and friends. It has taken decades, but the Latina on the silver screen has slowly evolved into a real person.

Luscious at Work

IN THE REAL world, Latinas are trying to decide if they can be lus-cious and still be taken seriously. Although the luscious Latina image may be more glamorous than that of a maid or spitfire, a stereotype is still a stereotype. It's great to be desired, but it's not so great to be con-sidered "easy" or "loose." More and more Latinas have entered the business arena, and in corporate America, the luscious Latina image is far from welcome or useful. In May of 1997, I explored this topic for *Hispanic* magazine. I found several Latinas who confirmed that the stereotype existed and that most Latinas celebrate their sex appeal rather than try to cover it up. "Considering the vast genetic mix that makes up most Latinos—from the indigenous to the Moors—it makes sense that we would be considered a physically attractive group of people," said Dr. Dorothy Caram, who was affiliated with the Institute for Hispanic Culture in Houston, Texas at the time. "For too long, Latinas have been discouraged from being assertive and self-confident.

I think it's good that we've gained confidence in our beauty so long as we show off our brains at the same time."

When interviewing Latinas for the article, I found one who captured the duality of the luscious Latina and used it for all its potential. She was a young professional and highly educated. Very much a public relations–type person, she attended several functions hosted by the magazine, and I got to know her well. She had a master's degree in public administration and was a National Urban Fellow at Baruch College in New York. Originally from Texas, this Latina said she faced several stereotypes. Tall, thin, and dark-skinned, with long, thick, curly hair, she did create a striking image. Her hair was a target for much of the criticism, she admitted, but rather than cut her hair, as Melanie Griffith did in *Working Girl*, she decided that her hair was a part of her identity. Rather than conform, she decided she would educate people about Latinas and the fact that many have brains as well as looks. "That's the problem, we don't have enough Latina role models in the media that combine beauty with intelligence. Growing up, I spent so much time concentrating on developing my intelligence that when people first started commenting on my looks, it surprised me," she said. "I feel more pressure to present a balanced view of Latinas, staying in the middle as opposed to letting one side take over—the business side or the feminine side."

LATINAS IN LOVE SURVEY

Q: What is your annual income?

A: Sixty-nine percent of the Latinas who responded earned between $30,000–$100,000.

Q: How many years of formal education do you have?

A: Sixty-nine percent had twelve to sixteen years (bachelor's degree), 30 percent had sixteen to twenty years (master's degree), 4 percent had over twenty years (Ph.D.) and 7 percent had six to twelve years.

In the end, the article received a lot of criticism. It was written to celebrate the modern Latina, but corporate Latinas who had struggled since the 1970s to work their way up the corporate ladder and into one of very few management positions available to them complained loudly. The cover, which featured Hayek, Carmen Miranda, and Charo, belittled Latinas, they said, and set them back. They wanted to see a more conservative image of Latinas as professionals in suits. That may work for some, but like it or not, Latinas can be sexy. The reaction to this article reflects the position many Latinas found themselves in, in the wake of the women's movement. They felt they had to deny their Latina-ness in order to be successful. What came naturally to them—their sex appeal—was not an asset but a liability, and an article that celebrated Latina-ness was seen as a threat to progress. *Hermanas*, we can be both.

The response to the "luscious" stereotype can be extreme. The concern about our "look" causes many writers to counsel Latinas to "blend in." For example, in *The Maria Paradox*, Drs. Rosa Maria Gil and Carmen Inoa Vazquez state, "We all know that our choices of colors, style of shoes, hair, and manicures have a lot to say about us as individuals and as Latinas.... However, if you wear a very bare, very floral, very mini sundress, big jewelry, stiletto heels, and long false fingernails with decals to school or to work in the winter, you'll be setting yourself apart from your fellow students and teachers or co-workers—an open invitation for them to judge you unfairly." Yet post-feminist Naomi Wolf admits that the double standard for women regarding how they are perceived in the office based on what they wear does exist. In her book *The Beauty Myth* she writes: "Emulating the male uniform *is* tough on women. Their urge to make traditionally masculine space less gray, sexless, and witless, is an appealing wish. But their contribution did not relax the rules.... The consequence of men wearing uniforms where women do not has simply meant that women take on the *full* penalties as well as the pleasures of physical charm in the workplace, and can legally be punished or promoted, insulted or even raped accordingly."

There were no Latinas at the forefront of the women's movement, nor did the agenda address the issues of women of color. Since the women's movement didn't appear to include them, some Latinas feel less obligated to abide by its rules. Latinas revel in their femininity, and they're not going to downplay it. The modern Latina may not wear a black suit to work every day, but that doesn't mean she's not as dedicated to her work as the next co-worker. At work, lusciousness tends to be suppressed, but it can surface.

LATINAS IN LOVE SURVEY

Q: Do you support the movement for equal rights for women?

A: Ninety percent of those surveyed said they support the women's movement "absolutely." When asked if the women's movement included women of color, 60 percent said "Yes."

Even though its rhetoric and its membership did not overtly embrace Latinas, the women's movement has affected them. Latinas today are more ambitious, successful, educated, and talented than their predecessors were, and they continue to rise higher than ever before in the corporate and political world. Their progress is as much a reflection of growing self-confidence as a sign of the times. Latinas do embrace the women's movement and celebrate changes women have achieved. They want a better life for themselves and their children and have entered the workforce in order to get it. Although their mothers may have been shy and less likely to demand equal treatment at work, modern Latinas have a much lower tolerance for injustice and will speak up. They're educated, they're professionals, and luscious or not, they demand respect.

To truly be free, Latinas have to be proud of who they are. But remember, *chicas,* sex appeal is not an open invitation for sexual harassment. Not all men know this, however, and so rather than being someone that you're not, Latinas should just use good judgment at the office. Every office has its own dynamic, and your inner voice will tell you what will fly and what won't.

Luscious Side-Effects

WHAT DOESN'T WORK in the office can most certainly be an asset in the bedroom. But even when it comes to sex, the duality of perception versus reality can also be tricky for many Latinas. Latinas have evolved from a diverse gene pool and are raised with a rich cultural heritage. As an added bonus, the added melanin some of us have in our skin staves off many signs of aging so that we look much younger than we actually are. We generally have a distinctive fashion sense and love color. We're comfortable with the concept of flirting, and we move with a natural sensuality. Our skin color ranges from *morenitas* (dark-skinned), *mulattas* (Afro-Latinas), *güerdas* (fair-skinned), and *rubias* (very fair-skinned). Our looks have been called exotic, but whatever the reason, when a Latina walks into a room, she turns heads. Overshadowing all of this, however, is an insecurity that Latinas don't represent the beauty standard in this country reflected in Hollywood or in fashion and beauty magazines. With publications like *Latina*, *Latina Style*, and *Estylo*, some of that is changing, but the effects of rarely seeing ourselves on television, in film, and in print will take some time to overcome.

Outside of Hollywood, the luscious Latina image speaks to a Latina's self-confidence. Those who wear it as a badge believe it gives them an advantage, especially in love. They won't let it work against them. Other Latinas, however, see it as an encumbrance and will work diligently to destroy it. Some Latinas are uncomfortable with the luscious perception because although it's nice to be seen as sexy, the downside is that sexy can mean easy. The reality, however, is Latinas are rarely easy. Good Catholic girls, for the most part, we are trained at an early age to just say no. It's still not uncommon for Latinas to experience the anxiety of their first sexual experience on their wedding nights, as well as the disappointment that their husbands did not turn out to be the sex god that an "experienced" man was supposed to be.

Latinas did not ignore the sexual revolution. As they took on the battle for equality at the office, they also began the first step toward equality in the bedroom by seeing themselves as sexual beings. The next step was to ask questions and actually talk about sex. Normally, knowledge is power, but Latinas continue to struggle with reconciling sexual freedom with honoring their parents and the church.

LATINAS IN LOVE SURVEY

Q: What is your religion?

A: Seventy percent of the Latinas surveyed were Catholic.

Luscious in the Bedroom

VIRGINITY HAS BEEN overrated for centuries, but in the last few decades, that began to change. Nowadays it appears that virginity is underrated. We are very influenced by what we see on TV, and the message of many shows is: Have a lot of sex and learn to "think like a man." Many women truly believe that they should bring out the oversexed *Cosmo* gal inside them, but they forget that Helen Gurley Brown, the magazine's former editor, is a happily married woman. Women erroneously think that if they could learn to have sex like a man, maybe then relationships wouldn't be so difficult. The problem with that is women are not men. Books like *Men Are from Mars, Women Are from Venus* by Dr. John Gray confirm that idea. As Dr. Phil McGraw puts it: "Men and women are just wired differently."

As mentioned, scientists have discovered that women produce the same hormone during sex as they do during labor and while breast-feeding, which helps them bond with their babies as well as their sex partners. In a 1997 study conducted by zoologist Sue Carter at the University of Maryland, research was done on prairie voles, one of nature's more monogamous mammals. Carter found that when under normal circumstances female voles are able to bond, they do so with a two-day long sex romp, which releases the chemical oxytocin in the female. If deprived of oxytocin, she finds no male vole more attractive than another. When injected with the chemical, she will bond with whatever male she's with, whether or not they have already mated. "Researchers are beginning to sort out how body and mind work together to produce the wild, tender, ineffable, feelings we call love," writes Shannon Brownlee in a 1997 article in *U.S. News and World Report.* "They have found, for example, that oxytocin, a chemical that fosters the bond between mothers and children, probably helps fuel romantic loves as well. Brain chemicals that blunt pain and induce feelings of euphoria may also make people feel good in the company of lovers." To trigger the release in humans, all that's required is a loving touch. "Touching sparks a surge in oxytocin, which is secreted from the posterior section of the pituitary gland as hormone-like chains of molecules called peptides. The estrogen-dependent chemical flows to various receptor sites in the brain and through the reproductive tract in both men and women (although women have bigger doses, which may explain the widely held belief that women want cuddling and men want sex)," explains Trish Snyder in a 1996 article in *Chatelaine.* "As well as promoting touch, it encourages bonding, triggers mild let-down during breastfeeding and sets off the uterine contractions that accompany childbirth and orgasm. All these events prompt oxytocin levels to rise in turn, creating a biochemical high akin to a subtle alcohol buzz."

When she heard about oxytocin, one twenty-something Latina I know, who professes to be very sophisticated when it comes to sex but has had a horrible track record in relationships, sarcastically quipped: "That just means that one-night stands are okay because then you won't bond. If you have sex with the same guy for a long period of time, then you'll start to bond and that's when you get hurt." Brilliant (now I'm being sarcastic). The objective should not be to get to know a lot of weenies but rather, to get to know the guy first.

In her book *Getting to "I Do,"* Dr. Patricia Allen warns against casual sex. "Most liberated, sexually active women . . . believe they can maintain self-centered control over their emotions after sex. What they don't realize is that casual, noncontracted sex in a normal woman triggers a bonding that verges on physical addiction. This is due to a sexually stimulated hormone called oxytocin." Allen also separates men and women into masculine men, masculine-energy women, feminine women, and feminine-energy men. As the terms imply, masculine men will want relationships with feminine women who, she says, "prefer to be cherished than respected." Masculine-energy women may find feminine-energy men who will be less threatened by their success or independence, and therefore more compatible. "Just because you are a masculine woman and feel 'in control' of the relationship does not mean that you can have casual sex like a masculine man. Unless your are totally 'in your head' and out of your body, you will be affected by the hormone oxytocin. . . . So, just like a more feminine woman, you must check out your man before making love to him. Take time to find the right man so that you can have both a career and a loving partner."

In the bedroom, Latinas need to combine all the good messages from the women's movement with their natural instincts. You may be a natural seductress, but at the same time, you may have an incredible urge to please. That's fine as long as you make sure to get yours too! If a Latina learns early what she wants, and yes, I am talking about the m-word, masturbation, it makes things a lot easier when she has a partner. One of my favorite shows is the *Sunday Night Sex Show*, a Canadian program that is rebroadcast on the Oxygen channel. The host, sex educator Sue Johansen, gets calls from men asking how they should best please their lovers. "I don't know. Ask her," she responds. "Every woman is different, so you need to ask her what she wants, and if she can't tell you, then she needs to do her homework and masturbate and then tell you." In her *Book of Love, Sex, and Relationships*, Dr. Ana Nogales puts the issue in Latina terms, somewhat demurely: "It is so important for us to admire our own uniqueness and to love it. Learn to love what we've got, whatever that may be. Because some women tend to feel that their body exists primarily to be given to their partner, it's important to establish that sense of ownership. A woman needs to own her body before she can fully share it with her companion."

Latinas are much more comfortable with the concept of virginity, however, than with masturbation. Some modern Latinas have tried to live up to new sexual mores like more is better, but some also understand that virginity can be a valuable tool rather than a burden. It really helps weed out a lot of frogs. Consequently, Latinas do tend to wait longer than most women do. The average age most women lose their virginity is sixteen. Latinas tend to hold out a little longer. I'm not convinced that one-night stands are necessary, but at the same time, the days when a woman's first sexual experience arrives on her wedding night should be a thing of the past. Sex on the wedding night can often be more traumatic than romantic, especially if the groom turned out to be a dud. The fact that women are more comfortable today with their sexuality is a good thing, but the theory that they need to learn to have sex like a man is asinine. It also goes against nature.

LATINAS IN LOVE SURVEY

Q. At what age did you lose your virginity?

A. The average age that the Latinas who completed the survey claimed to have lost their virginity was eighteen to nineteen.

Ask most Latinas about the stereotype of the luscious Latina and you'll get a knowing nod with an acknowledging smile. Women have wielded sex appeal as a weapon for years and the fact that Latinas are considered sensual has its advantages. The basic attitude among Latinas seems to be: "We know it exists, and we like it." Although the image was originally negative—the Latina spitfire—somehow, this stereotype has changed over the years, to where it is embraced by many Latinas as a compliment rather than a slur. As actresses like Hayek continue to succeed in serious roles, more Latinas will reap the benefits of that success. The joke may be on Latinas who forget that the stereotype can include misperceptions, like sexual promiscuity or a lack of intelligence, but considering the reality—that Latinas have combined sexuality with intelligence for years—we still have the last laugh.

5

Latinas Online

The modern Latina uses modern technology to find love

Dear Amiga Mía,

I'm so glad you've gone online. I have looked for a chat room or a place where I could share my feelings in a Latino environment, but the options are very limited. Thanks to Hispanic Online for its wonderful Web page and for including your column. I don't have a specific problem to discuss at this time but I'm glad to know you're there when I do.

Maria, 25

$\mathcal{M}$Y EXPERIENCE AS an advice columnist has shown me that Latinas need to talk about their relationships now more than ever. In cyberspace, Latinas search for chat rooms and resources for helping with their romantic lives. Maria's sense of relief at finding someone to simply talk about love with is universal.

Falling in love is easy. Sometimes it happens with just a wink and a nod. More often than not, however, it develops gradually, almost subconsciously, and then suddenly it hits you in an amorous epiphany. Women read, fantasize, and dream about it from a very early age. No matter how liberated or modern, we are suckers for romance and dream that when we meet Mr. Right, it'll be just like in the movies. The fact that a book like Jane Austen's *Pride and Prejudice*, the quintessential romance novel, has never been out of print since it was first published in 1813 is proof of that. Written almost two hundred years ago, the book should have become outdated by now, but it tells the story of a classic romance—boy meets girl, boy and girl hate each other, boy and girl fall madly and passionately in love—that still resonates with people today.

Romance, especially in novels, is especially delicious because it encourages women to do what they do best, fantasize. What the books don't say explicitly, especially one written in 1813, we can imagine for ourselves. In our own lives and our own heads, we can make any relationship work and the sex is always fabulous. This may also explain the popularity of Harlequin romances. According to the Romance Writers Association, sales of these salacious stories remain strong, confounding literary critics worldwide. Almost one of every five books sold in the U.S. is a romance novel. Yes, we love romance, but in reality dating can be a drag and sometimes even meeting someone we'd consider dating seems impossible.

As young girls, we speculated with friends about who would be the man of our dreams. Like Snow White, we believed that some day our prince would come. Just the anticipation that it could be anyone, that it would be years before we ever knew whom, and that one day somehow, some way, our princes would find us, excited us.

Of course, we didn't know then that there would be many frogs along the way. Unlike the frogs in fairy tales that eventually turn into princes, these frogs start out as princes and develop warts as the relationship progresses. (Incidentally, the frog prince tale explains a woman's propensity to try to change her man.) Once these princes metamorphose into frogs, the evil toads have already wasted a lot of our time and stolen our hearts. Yes, falling in love is easy. But finding a prince among a lot of frogs is just a plot in a fairy tale.

The biggest challenge in romance for the modern female is meeting men. In the past, family, friends, and the church brought couples together. Surrounded by family and sanctioned by the church, the couple met, spent time together, and after a few years had passed, if both were so inclined, they married. With no prospects for work or a career, girls waited patiently for a man who could provide for them. Girls (many were teenage brides) had little choice in the matter and were married off. With few options available to them, these women were not just overworked, they were stuck, and the men weren't all princes by any stretch of the imagination. Some were mere brutes, and the lives of many housewives resembled nightmares, not dreams. Those days—when modern conveniences were few and women, preoccupied with housework and bearing children, were too overwhelmed to worry about having fun—are dwindling, at least in most industrialized societies. Some day, I hope, they will end for good.

As one century made way for another, women gained more rights and a little independence. Suddenly, they had choices in who they married, and women could marry for love instead of security. Women had to be courted, much like the princesses they read about in those early fairy tales. The word itself has a regal root, referring to the days when to be a member of the king's court was to be part of a group of people particularly selected to pay homage to the king. Similarly, a suitor had to pay homage to the girl. They brought flowers or a box of chocolates and tried their best to impress the female. Latino men serenaded their girlfriends, and in some countries, they still do. Back in the early to middle decades of the twentieth century, a man's intentions were clear—he was looking for a wife. A woman was seen as a prize, and a man had to be willing to be humiliated to earn her. Like Caesar, women had the option of giving a thumbs-up or thumbs-down. Of course, they had to be careful because if they chose the wrong guy, there would be no easy way out, and life in a bad marriage can seem interminably long. Devoutly, Latinas took the words "for better or worse," and "until death us do part," to heart.

LATINAS IN LOVE SURVEY

Q: Are your parents still married?

A: Seventy-eight percent of Latinas said that their parents were still married. Forty-seven percent of non-Latinas said that their parents were still married.

Over the decades, women gained more and more independence. Women won the right to vote, to own property, to get an education, to start a business, and to run for elected office. Consequently, women were able to choose qualities in a mate beyond financial security. Since women no longer needed men to support them, they looked for men who made good partners, companions, and lovers. For some, living with a guy instead of marrying him became a viable option.

Today the modern Latina doesn't have to see her future husband as a meal ticket; she can look for a soul mate, someone who really cares about her and is compatible with her personality. The days when she goes from her father's house to her husband's are over, and the responsibility for her future happiness is in her own hands. As her requirements for a life partner increase, however, the selection may decrease, and with no one to arrange it for her, meeting a mate gets complicated.

Women are much busier than they were in the past, so much so that socializing has to be scheduled. Also, much of their time is spent at the office and since the theory that an office romance is a bad idea has been proven more right than wrong, meeting people gets increasingly difficult. Many books suggest that women join clubs or volunteer in order to meet people, but who has time? Dating for the modern twenty-something woman gets replaced by partying, especially when those first post-college paychecks start rolling in. Once her career gets established, and the thirties commence, a woman may start to look for her life partner. By her mid-thirties, a woman's biological clock starts ticking, and the heat is on to reproduce. Actually, some women could probably wait longer, but infertility scares among older women have created a sense of urgency. But there's another theory, which has also come true more often than not, that you meet someone when you're not looking. Therein lies the rub. It seems like a girl can't win for trying, but there are alternatives. Modern problems require modern solutions, and many Latinas have solved the problem of meeting men by going online.

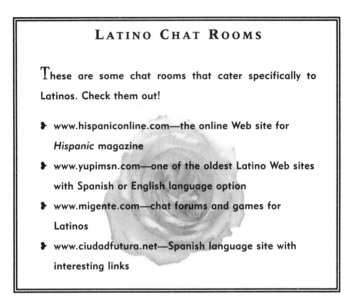

LATINO CHAT ROOMS

These are some chat rooms that cater specifically to Latinos. Check them out!

❥ www.hispaniconline.com—the online Web site for *Hispanic* magazine

❥ www.yupimsn.com—one of the oldest Latino Web sites with Spanish or English language option

❥ www.migente.com—chat forums and games for Latinos

❥ www.ciudadfutura.net—Spanish language site with interesting links

This so-called modern solution is really a flashback to a more romantic period when dating was done by correspondence. Couples got to know each other through letters rather than over cocktails. To have to put your thoughts and feelings down in words and do it romantically and artistically takes time and skill. For this reason, words in print are much more powerful than words in a conversation—it takes more effort to sit down and write than it does to blurt out a compliment or pick-up line. And words in print linger, providing proof of the author's love and admiration. Written words, whether a special note in a yearbook, a postcard, a ten-page love letter, or a romantic e-mail, will find a special place in a girl's heart. Spoken words, although thrilling, are impermanent. Once uttered, they evaporate, and over time, lose their resonance. The memory's embellishment helps, but the nagging desire to remember the exact words will persist.

Today, the prospect of getting to know someone, often sight unseen, is obviously appealing. "For many participants, virtual dating simply provides the thrill of the chase, a jolt of hormonal caffeine during a long workday or a lonely night," writes Brad Stone in an article in *Newsweek*. In the Latinas in Love survey, a forty-something non-Latina boasted: "I meet all my dates through the Internet," while a twenty-something, also a non-Latina, said: "I have met someone on the Internet. Didn't work out. Wouldn't do it again."

There have been horror stories, yes, but couples do meet successfully online. When this technological revolution began, many Latinos were at a disadvantage. The percentage of Latinos who were wired was far below that of other groups, and phrases like "digital divide" were used to describe the chasm between Latinos and the Internet. Recognizing that a diverse wired community was in their best interest, high-tech companies put computers in schools and public libraries and gave people incentives to purchase them for home use by lowering prices. Latinos did get up to speed and by the new millennium became one the fastest-growing Internet markets. In 2000, a report from Cheskin Research, a market research firm in California, found that 42 percent of the nation's 9.3 million Latinos had computers, a 68 percent increase from 1998. In 2001, Insight Research reported that Latinos and Asians are more likely to be online at home than

non-Hispanic whites and African Americans and that over the next
five years their Internet penetration rates will grow several times faster
than the rest of the population.

LATINAS IN LOVE SURVEY

Q: Would you consider meeting someone on the Internet?

A: Forty-eight percent of the Latinas who responded to
the survey said they would consider meeting someone
on the Internet, or had already tried it.

When it comes to love online, however, Latinas remain skeptical.
One thirty-something Latina admitted that she would consider meeting someone on the Internet, but cautioned, "I would think about it
for a long time." Usually naturally cautious, Latinas are dissuaded by
stories about women meeting rapists or children meeting pedophiles.
But since necessity is the mother of invention, when the normal
avenues for meeting people have not worked, many people, including
Latinas, have turned to the Internet.

With more Latinos getting wired, dating online also reached the
Latino community. Many Latino-themed chat rooms sprouted up, as
well as Spanish-language and bilingual Web sites. Dating services, such
as amigos.com, cater to Latino couples. The computer-savvy younger
generation was quick to explore chat rooms, but their lack of sophistication proved a bit risky. One of the letters I received as Pilar the

advice columnist was from a young Latina who told me about an online romance. Clearly in her teens, she was easily seduced by a boy's declaration of love and his desperate need to meet her. Unfortunately (or fortunately as it turned out), he lived in another state, but in her letter she said she was willing to chuck it all, move there, and attempt to start a life with him. I explained to her how meeting people online can be fun, but that you can't really know a person until you meet him in the flesh, and actually spend time with him. Long distance romances are also a bad idea, with or without the Internet. I successfully persuaded her to wait, take her time, and try to meet someone who lives in her town or at least within a fifty-mile range.

The Internet can be risky but if utilized correctly, and by more mature Latinas, it can work. I know of at least one Latina who did meet her future husband online. I'll call her Carol and her fiancé Chris.

Whether online or in person, the key to meeting compatible people is to look for people with similar interests. In person, you might join a club or volunteer for a cause or nonprofit organization. Online, you can find Web sites or chat rooms tailored to people with similar interests. A Latina and in her early thirties, Carol was quite comfortable with the Internet. She began her search by registering at an Internet dating service for Latinos called amigos.com. At the site, she listed her interests and what she was looking for in a potential boyfriend. Carol says, "I got a lot of responses, and some were a little weird. But I could tell, if a person expressed himself well, whether or not he might be interesting. One guy was pretty blunt, he just said, 'I know what women want. I've got a big penis and a big bank account.' I guess some women might respond to that, but I hit delete pretty quickly."

Meanwhile, Carol's future fiancé was living his life in the same city and about a mile away from her house. He had tried Internet dating without much luck. Chris admits that he dated a few women unsuccessfully, but he never misled them. His roommate, however, was quite another story. I'll call him Jake. Jake corresponded with several women online and each one believed that he was writing her exclusively. He even proposed marriage to a few of them. Once Jake established regular correspondence with a female, he would call her on the phone. Most of these women lived in a different state, so Jake eventually visited a few and enjoyed their company.

LATINO ONLINE ADVICE COLUMNS

Amiga Mía—written by yours truly in English
for Hispanic Online
Web site: www.hispaniconline.com.

Señorita Sentimiento—Spanish language column section
of Yupimsn.com
Web site: www.yupimsn.com/amor/consultorio.

Dolores Dice—advice column for *Latina* magazine,
posted to the online
Web site: www.latina.com.

Ask Coco—bilingual advice columnist Coco Helado writes
for Latino Matchmaker online dating service
Web site: http://match.pippin.dayton.in.us/advice.asp

Men who string along several women at the same time that they meet online are called "cyberscoundrels," or the male version of cyberhussies. The Internet's vastness can sometimes turn normal people into love hogs and flirt-aholics, captivated by the Internet's freedom and anonymity. Chris didn't realize the extent of the damage Jake had caused until after his roommate moved out. "One poor girl from Georgia kept calling for him. Finally, I told her that not only had he moved out but that he had left town and that I didn't know where he was. She was upset at first and that's when I found out that he had proposed to her and that she truly believed that they were getting married. I tried to comfort her and I guess it worked because the next thing I knew, she asked me, 'So what are you like?' Some people are really needy, and those are the ones who tend to make bad decisions, on or off the Internet," notes Chris.

Carol and Chris's story, however, is ripe with kismet. Carol's Latino singles site was apparently linked to Chris's non-Latino site. It had been months since he had received any referrals, and he had practically decided to give up on Web dating. "Then one day I got a referral to a girl who lived in my neighborhood, which shocked me. I think we were linked because in our bios we both listed language as an area of interest," Chris remembers. "It seems pretty random, but the fact that we met is also fate." Chris speaks six languages, including Spanish. Born in Mexico, Carol's first language is Spanish, but she is also fluent in English and speaks French.

They e-mailed each other a few times, and then Chris called Carol and arranged to meet her. "We chose a neighborhood coffee shop. Since we were both familiar with it, it gave us a comfortable, informal setting for a first date, and it's also a great place to talk," says Carol. Two years later, they got engaged. For this couple, the Internet gave fate a little push. They do, however, recognize that there are some dos and don'ts for those who try it.

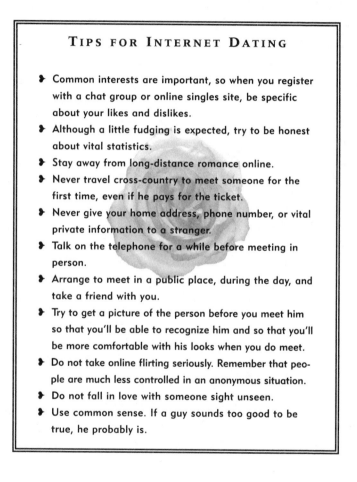

TIPS FOR INTERNET DATING

- Common interests are important, so when you register with a chat group or online singles site, be specific about your likes and dislikes.
- Although a little fudging is expected, try to be honest about vital statistics.
- Stay away from long-distance romance online.
- Never travel cross-country to meet someone for the first time, even if he pays for the ticket.
- Never give your home address, phone number, or vital private information to a stranger.
- Talk on the telephone for a while before meeting in person.
- Arrange to meet in a public place, during the day, and take a friend with you.
- Try to get a picture of the person before you meet him so that you'll be able to recognize him and so that you'll be more comfortable with his looks when you do meet.
- Do not take online flirting seriously. Remember that people are much less controlled in an anonymous situation.
- Do not fall in love with someone sight unseen.
- Use common sense. If a guy sounds too good to be true, he probably is.

Remember that as rare as love at first sight is, love at first byte is nearly impossible. Do not commit emotionally to any online friend until you have met him in person. As an online columnist, I received several letters from girls who had had online romances. It's easy to get carried away because flirting over the Web is easy and seems safe, but the mind will take a compliment or better yet, a declaration of love, and run with it, and that's when girls get into trouble. It's easy to lie when you don't have to say it to someone's face, and it's easy to create a fantasy, or embellish on reality when your relationship is based on words on the screen. "I think a lot of people are very lonely and have a hard time meeting people," says Carol. "Meeting people online is much less complicated and, at first, very easy. But, you have to remember that no matter how well a guy writes or expresses himself, the real test is meeting in person. If you've corresponded regularly and honestly online and then had a few phone conversations or even sent each other your photographs, the chances of being greatly disappointed when you do meet are much lower than, say, on your traditional blind date. Even still, the final test of whether the relationship is worth pursuing is if he turns you on, and you'll only find that out in person."

LATINAS IN LOVE SURVEY

Q: What traits are you looking for in an ideal mate?

A: Single Latinas listed honesty and sense of humor on their lists. Other popular traits were intelligence, kindness, being successful, and being romantic.

What Carol's referring to is chemistry. A cyberdate is really a blind date. Although most cyberdaters recommend that participants be as honest as possible because the truth will come out in the end, most participants do fudge about basic data like weight—by about ten pounds—and age—by about ten years. In a first-person account of her cyberdating experience in *Chatelaine* magazine, an unnamed author writes that she first entertained the concept as she was struggling through a divorce. She began with just a trial two-month free subscription to an online dating service, and although most of the men who contacted her were uninteresting, two interesting ones e-mailed her just as she was about to let her membership expire. She paid the thirty-dollar membership fee and continued the service. One man was a professor and the other was a composer. Both turned out to be duds, the composer especially, whom she consented to meet. He had sent a photo of a man with "a refined-looking face, touches of gray at the temples, a book in one hand, and more books lining the wall behind." In person, however, he was "in his seventies, with suspenders and old pants that hung below his pot belly."

After beating a hasty retreat, the writer admits that she still maintained her account, and a few of her friends also followed her lead. Again, just as her membership was about to expire, she decided to scan the profiles one last time and found a line from an e.e. cummings poem that she loved as a child. She decided to write to this prospect, and he responded, "immediately, with a lovely little e-mail that somehow moved me." The chase was on, and her mind took off. The fact that someone else felt the same way about an e.e. cummings poem, as opposed to Chinese food, for instance, clearly seemed "fated" to her. From that moment on, her mind took over. The two began corresponding on a daily basis. "The chemistry between us was electric, even across cyberspace," she writes. They took the next step and talked on the telephone for hours at a time. "How can you be falling in love with a man you've never met?" her friends asked. "I can talk to this man," she replied. "I feel as if I've known him for years."

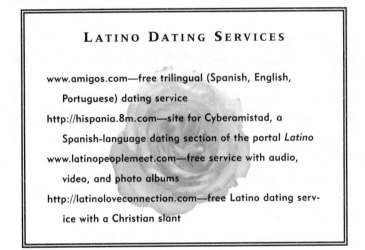

LATINO DATING SERVICES

www.amigos.com—free trilingual (Spanish, English, Portuguese) dating service

http://hispania.8m.com—site for Cyberamistad, a Spanish-language dating section of the portal *Latino*

www.latinopeoplemeet.com—free service with audio, video, and photo albums

http://latinoloveconnection.com—free Latino dating service with a Christian slant

Online chemistry is simply in the mind. "Skeptical observers of online dating . . . argue that the Internet doesn't convey the overall gestalt of a person, that impalpable physical essence that either carbonates your hormones or leaves them flat," writes Stone. "At the same time, the Net's limitations—no raised eyebrows or sarcastic smiles—can induce users to interpret e-mail more positively, while the anonymity of the medium tends to provoke premature personal confessions. The result is a positive-feedback loop."

Two months later, the moment of truth came and the poetic cyberdate traveled from Oregon to Toronto to meet Stone. The writer admits that she sent a younger photo of herself but did advise him to add a few years and pounds to the photograph. In person, however, he looked nothing like he'd described and was instead, "paunchy, flabby, unathletic, and decidedly unhandsome. I was shocked and cold with anger." After only one hour, he turned around and drove home. In retrospect, she remembered that she had liked him genuinely as a person and tried to communicate with him again but to no avail. The fact that she thought he was handsome, as well as extremely rich, colored her feelings. She was foiled not only by this guy's dishonesty—he had sent a fake picture—but also by her own imagination. Says Stone: "Seasoned online daters say that a satisfying way to pursue love on the Net necessitates a wholesale lowering of expectations."

On the positive side, however, cyberdating is a great cure for loneliness. For people who have recently moved to town, it's a great way to meet new people. Dating groups have also gotten more specific, which improves compatibility. Like the site created exclusively for Latinos, there are also sites for other ethnic groups. One site caters only to graduates of Ivy League schools. The Internet is huge. With millions of subscribers and thousands of new ones signing up daily, you're almost guaranteed a few hits. Some women assume a quantity over quality approach, and they go out on cyberdates on a weekly, or even daily basis. It can be exhausting, but if the approach is casual and not about finding Mr. Right, it can also be entertaining. For women who have exhausted their dating options at work or among friends, the Internet can provide a vast supply of new prospects. As we age, fewer and fewer of our friends are single and we hardly see our married friends. But go online and there are hundreds of single people waiting to meet you.

Goodbye, loneliness. Hello, BigBoy243.

6

Adiós, Chulo

Latinas no longer choose Latinos exclusively as mates

Dear Pilar,

I've dated white guys all my life until my latest boyfriend, who is Latino. I love gringos, but I also missed being with someone who came from the same culture as me. The problem is that his machismo is beginning to show. My white boyfriends were rarely jealous, and they respected my opinions even if they disagreed. My new boyfriend has begun to expect things from me, kind of like I'm his mom—cooking for him, shopping for him, etc. I don't want to lose him, but I don't think I can be happy turning into my mom or grandmother. How can I get this man to move into this millennium?

Juanita, 36

I'VE SAID IT before, but it bears repeating: Falling love is easy, finding Mr. Right is the challenge. For the modern Latina like Juanita, dating, courting, and marriage are more complex than ever. Her mother very likely married the boy next door, and her grandmother probably married the son of a close family friend. For most, the concept of an "arranged marriage" no longer exists. She can't rely on marrying a friend of the family. She's self-sufficient, accomplished, and independent, and she hopes to meet a man who is not only similarly equipped but who also respects and admires her for who she is. In contrast, her grandmother and mother looked for a man who could support a family first, over sex, compatibility, even love. Couples in arranged marriages didn't fall in love—they grew to love each other. The modern Latina hopes to marry for love above all else, but she also approaches marriage as a partnership and will consider a potential mate's compatibility with her personality, values, and culture as well as his fiscal responsibility. Once the more practical consideration of money is minimized, women create a fantasy mate, which leads to greater expectations. For her mother and grandmother, that man would invariably be Latino. For the modern Latina, that man could be anyone. Having such an open field increases the challenge of finding that perfect guy.

LATINAS IN LOVE SURVEY

Q. How would you rank the following components of a marriage—communication, equality, tenderness, money, sex, romance, children, honesty, excitement, love, humor, and compatibility—in order of importance?

A. Poll respondents ranked "love" highest, with "communication" coming in a close second. "Children" received the lowest, or least important, ranking, followed by "money."

Latina playwright Josefina Lopez once told me, "All successful Latinas marry white men." These may be fightin' words to many Latinas, but at the same time this overgeneralization does have a ring of truth. That's not to say that to be successful a Latina has to marry a white guy, but it does reflect the fact that many Latinas are not marrying Latinos. My husband is not Latino and neither is my sister's husband. Of my married Latina girlfriends, half married Latinos and half married non-Latinos. The 2000 U.S. Census reports that the greatest interethnic coupling takes place between non-Hispanic whites and Latinos. According to the Census, there are nearly two million couples in which one partner is of Hispanic origin and one is white. In comparison, there are about 700,000 white-Asian couples and about 450,000 black-white couples.

In 2001, *The Washington Post*, the J. Kaiser Family Foundation, and Harvard University teamed up to perform a survey of interracial couples. They found that of all the interracial groups, Latino-white couples reported the least difficulty finding acceptance of their union by family and society. Interestingly, the survey also found that whites were the least open to interracial marriage. Forty-six percent responded that it was better to marry within one's race, compared to 23 percent of Latinos, 21 percent of African Americans, and 30 percent of Asians who said it was better to marry "your own." When it comes to dating, many couples are venturing beyond their own cultural comfort zone. Among Latinos, the men are more adventurous. In the Harvard survey, 55 percent said they had dated other races, while 36 percent of Latinas said they had dated non-Latinos. Still, Latinas are embarking on new territory and not just with white men. They are also marrying men from other races, including African Americans and Asians.

Why would a Latina find someone not of her own culture more appealing, and what are the dynamics of an interracial marriage? If a Latina chooses to marry a Latino, what should she expect from a modern Latino marriage?

LATINAS IN LOVE SURVEY

Q: Are Latinos more, less, or equally as romantic as non-Latinos?

A: Forty-three percent of Latina respondents claimed that Latinos are more romantic than non-Latinos, 38 percent said that they are equally as romantic, and 11 percent said that Latinos are less romantic than non-Latinos.

Latino Husbands—For Better or Worse

LET'S START WITH the good stuff, namely, the Latin lover. Much like the luscious Latina image, the Latin lover ideal is a double-edged sword, but for the most part, the positive outweighs the negative. Latinos can't help but enjoy the perceived advantage they have over non-Latinos in the bedroom. In many situations, like being passed over for a job promotion or being refused for a bank loan, Latinos are expected to swallow their pride (the situation for Latinas is even worse when it comes to job security, promotion, and equal pay). But in the bedroom, they hold an advantage. True or not, being labeled an ideal lover isn't a bad thing when it comes to hooking up. There may be added pressure to live up to the image, but Latino men consider it a matter of cultural pride and gladly take on the challenge. Possibly, the only Latinos who take offense to the term are those in Hollywood. Just like their Latina colleagues, the roles offered Latino actors have been limited to this stereotype, or the other extreme of criminals, usually drug kingpins or gang members. But the Latino in the real world will use the Latin lover image for all he can. That said, is there any real truth to the rumor?

Again, it depends on the generation. Generally, the closer a Latino derives from Mexico, Latin America, the Caribbean, or Spain, the more he exhibits this quality. The more generations a Latino is a native of this country, the more he will adopt dating rituals of the U.S. A Latino from Argentina, for example, will be much more adept at courting than his fourth- or fifth-generation cousin will be. He'll be grandiose in his wooing and will have a flair for seduction. He'll be expert at using compliments and not shy about it. He knows that women are seduced by actions, words, and most importantly, their own heads. He'll call the object of his affections *corazón, amorcita, mi amor, mi reina,* or *mi vida.* When a man makes a woman feel like she's the only woman on the planet, he knows that a woman can't help but lose her balance. Latinos recognize this; they've practiced their techniques, and carry it off very well. For the woman who likes being swept off her feet, a Latino is the man for the job.

Dr. Ana Nogales, author of *Dr. Ana Nogales' Book of Love, Sex, and Relationships* concurs. "Even after marriage, most Latinas (and non-Latinas!) require that the romantic aspects of the 'Latin lover' be present if they are to be fully aroused. The stereotypical boastful lover who counts his numerous conquests or judges his sexual success according to how long he can sustain sexual penetration usually holds little interest for women. But the romantic lover whose aim is to focus his full attention on the woman he loves, who appreciates her and who takes the time to find out what takes her breath away—this kind of 'Latin lover' will be rewarded with the reciprocal love of a passionate 'Latina lover.' A woman wants a man to make her feel, through all the things that come before sexual intercourse, that she is exquisitely loved."

The women's movement had its good points, but it also brought about changes that many Latinas find offensive. Gentlemanly behavior—opening doors, pulling out chairs, paying for dinner—was suddenly questioned. Could women expect men to defer to them in this way and then still treat them as equals? Apparently not. But many Latinos stick with their traditions. In general, a female will rarely have to face the question of whether or not she should pick up the tab or "go Dutch" on a date with a Latino. A Latino wouldn't think of it. He was raised by a Latina, remember, so he has a certain respect or deference for women. This attitude will be carried on for several generations, but a fourth- or fifth-generation Latino, or one who was born in the seventies or eighties, may question this tradition and adopt a more modern approach. The worst thing any man can do is to throw the women's movement in his date's face when she complains about his manners. If younger Latinos and non-Latinos make that mistake, I hope they'll also learn from it. As a rule, Latinos will be courteous and gentlemanly on a date. They will open doors, help you on with your coat, keep pace with you, and pick up the tab. Heterosexual Latinos *love* women, and it shows. They don't fear them or resent them. They do, however, respect them. Of all the arts of seduction, this is the most effective. A woman can sense this attitude in a man, and it's intoxicating.

Latinos may enjoy the Latin lover stereotype, but as with all stereotypes, there is a downside. In this case, it's the assumption that Latinos love women so much they have to have many women. The assumption that a Latino will be unfaithful, more so than non-Latinos, has yet to be proven, but what was discovered in *Sex in America*, a survey conducted in 1994, was that Latinos and Latinas were more familiar with the concept of infidelity. University of Chicago sociologist Edward Laumann surveyed 3,500 people, 300 of whom were English-speaking Latinos. He concluded that the rate of infidelity among Hispanics in the United States was equal to the rate of infidelity for the U.S. population and that the stereotype of Latinos being more unfaithful than non-Latinos was exaggerated. Overall Laumann found that 15 percent of married women had had an extramarital affair while 25 percent of married men had been unfaithful. In a 1995 article in *Hispanic* magazine, Ines Pinto Alicea interviewed a Miami-based sex therapist, who concluded that infidelity among Latinos is more common for newer arrivals than multi-generational Latinos. By the second or third generation, he said, infidelity was not as much of an issue.

LATINAS IN LOVE SURVEY

Q: Are Latinos more, equally, or less modern than non-Latinos?

A. A small majority of Latinas in the survey (51 percent) said they were less modern, 47 percent said that they were equally modern, and 2 percent said that Latinos were more modern than non-Latinos.

Even though the majority of women surveyed answered that Latinos were less modern than non-Latinos, the Harvard interracial survey did find that Latinas and non-Hispanic white women were the least likely to date a different race. Only one-third of those surveyed admitted to dating outside of their race. As Latinas, we are naturally protective of our Latino brothers. We're tired of hearing *gringos* mispronounce and misuse the word *macho*. We're offended by the stereotype that all Latinos walk around in wife-beater t-shirts, swill beer in front of the television, and shout out, "*Vieja, trae me otra cerveza.*" Yes, machismo is a term used to describe an exaggerated sense of masculinity that's usually displayed in men who tend to dominate the females in their lives. The fact that the word is Spanish may explain why Latinos are often labeled macho. But machismo is just a state of mind. Some men have it, some don't, and it can occur in men of any color. Guys have testosterone, the source of all machismo. It's useful in certain situations, but too much of anything is never good. The question in my survey wasn't meant to refer to machismo. It was meant to uncover how the modern Latina perceives the modern Latino and how he stands intellectually when it comes to the women's movement and relationships.

Although many Latinos are hip to the new millennium and appreciate a Latina's independence, career, and modern attitude, a few still want a wife who will perform the traditional duties expected of her—cook the food, wash the dishes, provide regular sex, take care of the baby—in short, stay home. Some recognize that Latinas are now viable wage earners and will not oppose their wife's desire to have a career, yet they may still maintain their traditional expectations, which means she is expected to do all of the above in addition to keeping a full-time job.

Heaven help the Latina who marries a Latino who says she reminds him of his mom. She'll either be placed on a pedestal, eventually becoming untouchable, or she'll spend much of her time competing with *la madre*. The source of this dysfunction is usually the male-centered mom, a woman who calls her son *mi rey*, and caters to his every need while expecting her daughters to cook, sew, and wash their brother's clothes! These guys are the dreaded *mijos* (mamma's boys) and should be avoided. We can't fault anyone for loving his mother, but we can fault these ladies for creating *mijos*. They will not be compatible with the modern Latina bride, and their mothers will be the *suegras* from hell. Nothing you do will be good enough for her son, and you'll have to take her criticism because the *mijo* cannot accept that his mother is anything but perfect. He also cannot accept responsibility for anything. He was treated as a prince and therefore expects all his messes to be cleaned up—by you. One of my survey respondents admitted that the worst advice her mother ever gave her about marriage was that if a man treats his mother well, it's a sign that he'll treat you well. She says: "I found that 'mommy' is still number one while I am a distant second, maybe even third. He may treat me well, but the romance factor is not there. As long as she's around, expect a big baby on your hands."

Marriage of Equals

LATINAS HAVE PROGRESSED professionally beyond their mothers and grandmothers. They have integrated the work force at the executive and managerial levels. They have read *Cosmopolitan* and have listened to Gloria Steinem and read *The Feminine Mystique* by Betty Friedan and *The Maria Paradox* by Rosa Maria Gil and Carmen Inoa Vazquez. Although the women's movement, for the most part, ignores the voices of women of color, the issues of equality and independence have struck a chord with Latinas. Today, Latinas want a career, as well as a marriage and a family. To do this, they need an equal partner, a man who will take up the slack when it comes to household chores or finances, a man who will not resent this but who considers it his duty to make the partnership work. In our marriage, my husband and I share most of the chores. For example, he cooks, because he's better at it, and washes the dishes. I'm better at cleaning projects like bathrooms, dusting, and changing bed linens. I explained this once to a Latina friend and she responded, "Wow. You could never be married to a Latino."

However, a partnership isn't all a Latina wants. She also very much wants romance, and Latinos are strong in this department. Some have better technique than others do, but what gives Latinos an advantage is their attitude—from the courtesy they show women to the way they make love. Although a partner is important, a Latina still wants a man to court her, not negotiate with her. She also wants to keep her cultural ties alive, especially when it comes to her children, and that will probably include speaking at least some Spanish. No matter the generation, eventually Spanish will be introduced into the home. A Latina will take classes to brush up if she has to. Her life partner will have to accept this, and ideally, join with her to encourage a bilingual household. Naturally, a Latino will compliment rather than obstruct a Latina's need to keep her culture alive, and for many Latinas, this attribute is extremely important.

For years, Latinos have struggled over what term they prefer regarding their ethnicity. Are they Hispanic or Latino, or Puerto Rican or Nuyorican or Mexican American or Chicano? Many non-Latinos have made an effort to be sensitive to the fact that whatever term a person uses is a distinctly personal decision. This country is still adjusting to its changing demographics. People from an ethnic minority and those who are part of the mainstream majority will always have different perspectives on race because they experience it from different sides of the fence. Understandably and inevitably, Latinas and non-Hispanic white boys will have this discussion if they end up as a couple. Because Latinas fear that this conversation might get ugly, they may opt to avoid it by not dating men outside of their race, sticking with the familiarity of "their own."

In the Latinas in Love survey, women were not only asked to give their preference in a mate between Latinos and non-Latinos, but also to give a reason. One Latina responded that she preferred Latinos because "I live a relatively 'Latino' life and I don't want to be a tour guide through my culture." For some Latinas, marrying a non-Latino requires a sacrifice. Many times, cultural traditions will fade and Latinas may feel isolated or insecure the further they move from their cultural comfort zone. There's also the subtle fear that marrying into a non-Latino world will put a Latina at a disadvantage. Although it may occur less and less, she may have an underlying fear that she will be treated like a second-class citizen or that she'll be slapped in the face by a careless racist comment. For many Latinas, to give up some part of themselves in order to be compatible with men or to risk exposure to any kind of dehumanizing behavior or comment is just not worth it.

LATINAS IN LOVE SURVEY

Q. What is your ethnic preference for a mate?

A. Latino (56 percent), no preference (20 percent), non-Hispanic white (18 percent), and non-Hispanic black (6 percent).

Non-Latino Husbands—For Better or Worse

SOME LATINAS WHO choose non-Latinos marry an African or Asian American. With other men of color, Latinas will find similar cultural cues, such as respect for elders and tradition, and a social perspective that sees color (race, ethnicity) as a good thing and not a problem to be solved or ignored. Still, more Latinas marry whites than any other non-Latino group. Based on census figures, the biggest percentage of inter-ethnic marriages is between Latinos and non-Hispanic whites. It is a cultural leap, but for the modern Latina, the potential independence and equality she can find with a non-Latino is certainly tempting.

Many Latinas can pass for other ethnicities, such as French, Lebanese, or Italian. For some, this provides a safe haven, allowing them to be accepted before any ethnic consideration arises and avoiding potential negative reactions. For many, however, it requires that they constantly claim their identity and educate the world about who they are. The biggest barrier between Latinas and non-Hispanic white men is language, not race, and if they were raised in a part of the country with a large Latino population, neither the Latina nor her non-Hispanic white male husband view the union as interracial. In the Harvard survey, a white female respondent admitted that she never told her parents that her husband was Puerto Rican until after she was sure that her father liked him. "I think he just assumed he was Italian," she said.

Language creates a greater challenge for Latinas and non-Hispanic white males, but the more generations in the U.S. a Latina has, the less it is an issue. Latinas are in vogue, remember, and more and more, bilingualism is a bonus and not a flaw. As a columnist for Hispanic Online, I received a letter from a non-Hispanic white male who was worried that his daughter would miss out on her Latino culture. His wife, a first-generation Latina and non-Spanish speaker, and his in-laws, Mexican natives and Spanish speakers, were uninterested in perpetuating the language and more concerned with being "American." But he wanted his daughter to be bilingual, bless his heart. I advised him to take Spanish classes and shame his wife into joining him, and if the grandparents didn't oblige him by sharing their native language with their granddaughter, to get his daughter a Spanish-speaking babysitter. He believed that his daughter's ethnicity was an asset, and this kind of attitude among non-Hispanic white males can help make them suitable mates for modern Latinas.

Whether or not Spanish is a Latina's first or second language won't necessarily cause or prevent culture clashes with her non-Latino husband. This country has progressed since the decades when the Texas Rangers lynched Latinos, but it wasn't long ago that many Americans expressed anger and resentment at new Latino immigrants. As recently as the 1990s, Latinos were blamed for the country's economic problems, and California governor Pete Wilson instigated a damaging anti-immigrant campaign that triggered a Latino backlash and eventually helped pass three laws aimed at Latinos: Propositions 187 (anti-immigrant), 209 (anti-affirmative action), and 227 (anti-bilingual education). The fact that the Latino population has spread to parts of the country where people may have eaten Mexican food but never really seen a Mexican has also produced challenges. As a person of color, a Latina will be keenly sensitive to comments or actions that subjugate her.

> # LARGE LATINO GAINS
>
> States with the largest population increase were the south and southeastern U.S., regions that have traditionally had low Latino populations. States with the biggest growth in Latino population in the past decade were:
>
> North Carolina—393.9 percent
> Arkansas—337 percent
> Georgia—299.6 percent
> Tennessee—278.2 percent
> Nevada—216.6 percent
>
> *Source: 2000 U.S. Census*

Part of the appeal of white boys as partners is that they are forbidden fruit. For a Latina to marry outside of her ethnic group is a risk, and her parents know it. They fear that their daughter will be mistreated or unappreciated by her *gringo* husband and in-laws. For some Latinas, white boys are different from other ethnic groups. They come from a different world where (usually) skin color isn't a factor, and one less reason to be insecure just adds to their power. This country was established by white men, as were its laws, institutions, and in some cases, its churches. That historical dominance gives white males a unique self-assurance that is very alluring. By comparison, some Latino men carry a "chip on their shoulder" and a deep-seated resentment toward the dominant culture. That insecurity can be interpreted as a sign of weakness while the lack of it is perceived as a sign of strength, and we all know that power is the greatest aphrodisiac. Many women are attracted to strength and power because they need that sense of security. Non-Hispanic white men navigate more easily through society, especially in a professional arena, and they can help guide a young professional Latina, who has to live and work in the same society.

One survey respondent explained her attraction to white boys like this: "I've always been attracted to white boys because they're taller and less jealous or possessive." The height issue is a personal preference but there is one thing that non-Hispanic white men do understand, equality, and it may translate into being less jealous and possessive. Jealousy is also a sign of insecurity, and it's an unappealing trait in both sexes. The source of non-Hispanic men's more modern approach to relationships can also be attributed to history. The women's movement began with white women, and many young white men had mothers who were affected by it. They saw women attain more and more equality in all walks of life, and although their fathers may have resented it, these young men eventually accepted it. Today they appreciate the favors in the gift of women's liberation—a more independent female is self-sufficient and more fulfilled. Rather than depend on her husband, she'll be a partner in the marriage, putting less pressure on him to be the provider. When it comes to children, the partnership continues, with both parents actively involved with their children, from changing diapers to getting the kids to soccer practice.

In her book, *The Second Stage*, author Betty Friedan calls it the "quiet movement" of American men. "It is nothing like the women's movement, and probably never will be," she writes. "Each man seems to be struggling with it quietly—at twenty-five or thirty-five, or before it is too late, at forty-five or fifty. . . . He feels awkward, isolated, confused. Yet, he senses that something is happening with men, something large and historic, and he wants to be part of it. He carries the baby in his backpack, shops at the supermarket on Saturday, bakes his own bread with a certain showing off quality. . . . Some men just know they don't want to be like their fathers, or like those senior partners, who have heart attacks at fifty—but they don't know what other way there is to be." More than twenty years have passed since Friedan wrote her book and what she had begun to notice has since fully flowered into an acceptance of equal responsibility for the marriage partnership. This attitude naturally appeals to the modern Latina who wants an true partner in marriage. She doesn't want to role-play and revert to the same unempowered position of generations of Latinas before her. She likes being independent, and she wants a man who's going to encourage that. She may even opt not to change her name because after all, why should she? Chances are, a non-Latino will respect that decision too.

Equality is great, but it's not very romantic. Keeping track of who paid for dinner last or putting a price limit on Christmas or birthday gifts can get old. Remember, girls, we want romance. We want to live in a fairy tale or movie as much as humanly possible, so our guys will have to make an extra effort to keep us happy. After so much effort and time spent on accepting the women's movement and equality, white boys tend to resent it when women expect them to open the door or pick up the tab. Still, for women, much of romance is in the mind, so if a Latina finds a white boy who rings her bell, she'll blossom and he'll be a very lucky guy.

LATINAS IN LOVE SURVEY

Q: What's the most romantic thing your husband ever did for you?

A: "Take care of me when I am sick."

A: "Sang song in public to me."

A: "Bought me a dress just because."

A: "Planted roses for me so I could have flowers on a regular basis and think of him."

A: "He left a flower on the back windshield of my car and wrote backwards on the dirty window so that I could read from my rearview mirror, 'I love you my little dessert flower.' I read it when I got out of work late at night."

A: "I guess the most romantic thing was to surprise me on Valentine's Day. I was pregnant with our son and he was working out of town. I was a little down because I had to spend Valentine's Day alone. About nine P.M. the doorbell rang and there he was on the front porch with a Valentine's present. I was so surprised and happy that I cried. He had to get up at the crack of dawn to get back to his job which was a hundred miles away."

---

continued

A: "Once when he knew I was going to have a long,
rough day at work he was ready. When I got home
from work, he was making dinner and had candles,
wine, and had made arrangements to drop off the
children with my mother for the afternoon. He had
roses and massage lotion and gave me a great back
rub and had everything ready for me to take a relax-
ing bath while he picked up the kids and put them to
bed. It was wonderful and told me that he cared."

Latinas also know that among some non-Hispanic white males they
have greater cachet than among Latinos. Clearly, many Latinas prefer to
marry a fellow Latino, but unfortunately, they're not always available or
even interested in Latinas. Where there's comfort in a shared culture
there's also the downside of being taken for granted. When a Latina
meets that non-Hispanic white boy who's genuinely attracted to
Latinas, she will find him irresistible. It could be the luscious Latina
stereotype in action, but for some reason, Latinas disarm certain men,
and that's not only flattering, it's extremely appealing. In this situation,
Latinas are in charge, and that's a situation many women can't resist.

And don't forget, the boy's family will play a role in the relationship. Just as there are *suegras* from hell to deal with, a Latina might be
struck by the lack of communication and warmth she experiences

from her non-Latino in-laws. We're very touchy-feely people, but most non-Hispanic white families are not about showing emotion, which in many cases translates into a lack of affection. With continued exposure to Latino in-laws, however, some non-Hispanic white husbands may warm up to expressions of affection and openness, and learn to accept and even reciprocate the *abrazos* and *besos*. Latinas, on the other hand, may have to get used to no hugs, except on rare occasions like weddings or funerals, or no greetings at all. Don't be surprised if no one gets off the couch, comes to the door, or heaven forbid, interrupts their all-important game of Yahtzee to say hello when she and her husband (their son) show up at family gatherings.

What man will make the best match for modern Latinas? Are Latino men still stuck in the last generation? Can they be brought to more modern ways of thinking with a Latina at their side? And can a Latina be truly happy with a man outside of her own culture? The answer is yes to all of the above, it just depends on the Latina and what she wants. Who a Latina ends up with is her choice, and if maintaining cultural ties is a major priority, then she will find that she shares more in common with Latinos and will appreciate not having to explain her cultural motivation when she hangs a picture of the Virgen de Guadalupe on the wall. On the other hand, the Latina who considers herself very independent and modern may find that non-Latinos better complement that attitude, especially if they were raised by women who grew up with the women's movement and have learned to accept and respect independent, successful females. As human beings, nobody's perfect, but both Latinos and non-Latinos have much to offer the modern Latina. The choice is yours, *mi amiga*.

7

Latinas Who Love Too Much[1]

When a male obsession turns you into a love slave

Amiga Mía,

I have a friend who I think puts way too much value on what men think. When we go out, I worry if she doesn't get any attention from the guys at the club. It's like she needs a man to notice her to feel good about herself, and she's a beautiful girl! She's also got a great personality, but at the same time, when she's bad, she's very bad. She gets all upset, in public, and starts yelling at the men, calling them losers. I've tried to talk to her about it, but she says it's what her mother taught her. She says her mother told her to always look pretty and be thin so that she could get a man. I really want my friend to be happy but I'm not sure she can be if she's so messed up about what men think of her. How can I help her?

Sylvia, 21

YLVIA'S FRIEND SUFFERS from man anxiety. Another way to look at it is worrying about not getting enough of a good thing. We all know too much of a good thing is usually not good. For instance, too much junk food makes your skin break out, and too

[1] I am indebted to Robin Norwood for this idea, which she popularized in her book *Women Who Love Too Much* (1985).

much champagne makes you sick. What does too much love do? Quite simply, it completely messes up your personality.

Alas, there is such a thing as loving too much, and just like anything in excess, the consequences are dire. Latinas who love too much need to be needed, they seek male validation through any means possible, and they're oblivious to fact that their behavior is unhealthy. Their obsessive approach to love is rarely successful, yet they trudge forward, committing the same mistakes again and again. They play the part required to attract a man—that of compliant sex goddess—and then manipulate him psychologically to keep him. As little girls, they may have experienced some type of dysfunction in their family—alcoholism, drug abuse, or divorce—that left them with a sharp sense of insecurity. When their home life was shattered, these young women retreated, put up psychological walls, or stepped up, taking over the role of the adult to support the single parent with whom the family was left. Insecure to the core, they did this to gain approval from that remaining parent and to be assured by them that they wouldn't be abandoned. As women, they will transfer this need for approval and security from the parent to the opposite sex. They now believe that how men perceive them determines their worth. They are slaves to the idea and will not feel complete without a man in their lives. Consequently, these women will have a very high tolerance for anything their husband or boyfriend dishes out, from cheating to beating.

In her book *Women Who Love Too Much,* psychologist Robin Norwood explores this condition using case studies of her female patients as well as her own personal experiences. Self-diagnosed as a woman who loves too much, Norwood explains that like many women who suffer from this condition, she never thought that the problem was all that bad, despite her apparent unhappiness. She writes: "It is one of the ironies of life that we women can respond with such sympathy and understanding to the pain in one another's lives while remaining so blinded to (and by) the pain in our own. I know this only too well, having been a woman who loved too much most of my life until the toll to my physical and emotional health was so severe that I was forced to take a hard look at my pattern of relating to men."

The title of the book struck me as applicable to many Latinas. It seemed to describe many girls I had known whose friendships I had lost over stupid men. As a friend, in high school I was very motivated to stand up for my friends (maybe this is where my alter ego of Pilar was born). My friends and I entered the dating world together, and I felt it was imperative that we support each other. Perhaps it was because I had two older sisters or that I attended an all-girl Catholic high school, but even before I recognized the women's movement, I was all about Girl Power. I gave out advice in earnest but also learned that sometimes my friends just wanted someone to listen to them and that they wouldn't necessarily take my advice unless it suited them— guys, I later discovered, actually would take my advice. This is where the friendships faltered because I was young and strong-willed and didn't have patience for friends who didn't listen to me! I couldn't accept that my friends chose to stay with idiots who made them unhappy rather than listen to their friend who was trying to build up their self-esteem so that they could be happy. In the end, what struck me about my ex-girlfriends was how little they valued themselves. I stepped up when called upon as a friend. I told them not to let a man take them for granted and pumped up their egos with assurances that they were beautiful, special, smart, and the type of girl any guy would feel lucky to know. With approbation like that, no woman could turn around and fall back into the same one-sided, abusive relationship, right?

Well, in high school, many friends and I parted ways over this issue. In college, and with a few heartbreaks under my own belt, I realized that my true role as a friend was to listen and hopefully plant the seed for my friends to learn to value themselves—this experience would later serve me well as an advice columnist. Norwood's book put a psychological label on what I thought was just female frailty, and it's encouraging to know that women who love too much are not doomed to repeat the same mistakes, man after man after man.

LATINAS IN LOVE SURVEY

Q. What is your best asset? What do you think men consider your best asset?

A. The top three answers for best assets in their opinion among the Latinas surveyed were:

"intelligence," "sense of humor," and "personality."

The asset they thought men considered their best was (in this order): "sense of humor," "breasts," and "looks" and "intelligence," which tied for third place.

Latinas are not immune to this condition because Latino families are not immune to the types of dysfunction that create this syndrome. For many years, women who loved too much were probably considered pathetic females with bad taste in men who never learned from their mistakes and were doomed to repeat them. They may have been called sluts as well because women with this condition tend to use sex as a means of attracting and maintaining the relationship. This behavior is not rational, but irrational. These women are addicted to love. Norwood writes: " . . . many, many of us have been 'man junkies' and like any other addict, we need to admit the severity of our problem before we can recover from it. . . . We give our love in the desperate hope that the man with whom we're obsessed will take care of our fears. Instead, the fears—and our obsessions—deepen until giving love in order to get it back becomes a driving force in our lives. And because our strategy doesn't work, we try, we love even harder. We love too much."

If you recognize yourself in these words, don't despair. There's hope. The first step is to analyze why you love too much, then look at ways to change your behavior, and finally review methods of combating this condition, beginning with building up your self-confidence. In women who love too much, self-confidence is often shattered early in their lives by a dysfunctional family dynamic. Latinas with low self-confidence will be the most vulnerable to unhealthy relationships. Latinas must battle for confidence on two fronts: against an established beauty standard that rarely looks Latina and against a culture that still gives males clout and promotes women's saintly mission to suffer for the family. Latinas will need to battle internal urges to remain meek, mild, and obliging. After so many years of obedience, denial, and abuse, can a Latina who loves too much change the way she sees herself? Yes, once *she* chooses to make the change.

Misery Loves Company

SOME GIRLS MAY be "boy crazy," but women who love too much are "men obsessed." As with any obsession, the behavior it inspires makes no sense except to the person who's obsessed. According to Norwood, women who love too much become obsessed with men because they are in fact obsessed with being loved. In her experience as a therapist, she began to notice a pattern among her female patients. Several had a similar complaint: they did not choose wisely when it came to men. Through therapy, she found that these women also shared a similar dysfunction as children: they were deprived of love or attention from one or both parents. In some cases, the parents divorced, robbing them of one parent and forcing them to "grow up too fast." At a very young age, they took on the role of confidante to the single parent and pseudoparent to the younger siblings. In some instances, the battling parents stayed married but competed for the child's affection. In other cases, one or both parents suffered from some kind of addiction, such as alcohol or drugs, and the child took on the role of caregiver to the parents and siblings.

> Think about your own friends—How do you think their childhoods affect their current romantic relationship, or lack therof? What about your own childhood?

The sense of security is shattered in these households, so the children develop a permanent fear that the home will be destroyed at any time and subsequently commit to doing whatever they can to maintain the status quo. Female children learn to protect others rather than themselves and later seek out a male who provides a similarly volatile home life, one she knows how to handle from experience. She feels more comfortable being the calm in the storm than a partner in a healthy, confident, communicative relationship. Women who love too much will naturally be attracted to men who have intimacy or substance abuse problems, who need mommies, and who will provide a home full of dysfunction. As an interesting aside, many women who love too much will have food rather than substance abuse issues, from overeating to anorexia.

These women are so used to bad relationships that they tend to maintain problems rather than solve them. They need to be needed, so if the dysfunction goes away, they feel unsettled, in a panic, because they're just not used to "normal." Consider the case of the woman who is married to an alcoholic. You may know her—she claims that her husband's substance abuse is the problem, but when he attends an Alcoholics Anonymous meeting and begins his own road to recovery, it doesn't help the woman's situation—it simply aggravates it. Eventually, the husband moves out because he realizes that his relationship with his wife is "driving him to drink." The prospect that her husband would no longer "need" her drove this woman to panic. Rather than bring harmony to the family, his sobriety causes her to pick fights and escalate the tension between them. Can a marriage like this be saved? Perhaps not, but maybe the woman's approach to the relationship can change. One of the ways it can change is if the woman (codependent in this alcoholic scenario) goes to Al-Anon. If she does this, she may learn that to be the spouse of an alcoholic is to be an addict as well. The spouse of the addict is sometimes addicted to being needed, so when the addict overcomes his problems, becoming stronger and more independent, the spouse panics. In order to accept his sobriety, she has to learn to accept herself, become independent, and take control of her own happiness and not try to control the happiness of others.

LATINAS IN LOVE SURVEY

Q. What do you consider to be your worst fault? What do you think men consider your worst fault?

A. The top answers Latinas gave were that they felt they were (in this order): temperamental, opinionated, too easy, busy, unaffectionate, and bossy. They thought men considered their worst fault to be (in this order): opinionated, no idea (no answer), temperamental, and bossy.

If love equals pain and distress, then Latinas who love too much will naturally seek bad boys, men who not only maintain an emotional distance, but also abuse them mentally and even physically. They avoid nice guys, and if they happen to become involved with one, they're unimpressed. Because they've relied on a feeling of dread to guide them for so long, they can't trust or get excited about a relationship without it. To these women, normal just doesn't feel right. A normal relationship feels boring. It lacks the excitement, panic, and explosiveness of the dysfunctional relationship. Women who love too much associate the feeling of panic in the pit of the stomach, or nervous anticipation, as a sign of love, so unless they're miserable, they won't believe they're really in love. Associating dread with love reflects back to that dysfunctional childhood, and since part of the motivation for loving bad men is an opportunity to right those childhood wrongs, these women learn to prefer the pain.

The thrill of the chase also consumes these women, and the challenge of "fixing" a dysfunctional man's life entices them. They have no interest in "normal" guys or anyone who's got his life together. They go from man to man, boyfriend to boyfriend, husband to husband, each with the same disastrous result. They're miserable, they know it, but they just can't stop themselves. According to Norwood: "Loving too much does not mean loving too many men, or falling in love too often, or having too great a depth of genuine love for another. It means, in truth, obsessing about a man and calling that obsession love, allowing it to control your emotions and much of your behavior, realizing that it negatively influences your health and well-being, and yet finding yourself unable to let go. It means measuring the degree of your love by the depth of your torment."

SELF-HELP RESOURCES
FOR LATINAS

1. *The Latina Bible* by Sandra Guzman
2. *The Maria Paradox* by Rosa Maria Gil, D.S.W. and Carmen Inoa Vazquez, Ph.D.
3. *Dr. Ana Nogales' Book of Love, Sex, and Relationships* by Dr. Ana Nogales

---

For the men loved by these women, there are definite advantages. She's basically a "love slave" and will do anything to make her man happy. She will forgive infidelity, she will overlook his slacker attitude, and work even harder to support the family. "Women who love too much have little regard for their personal integrity in a love relationship," writes Norwood. "She'll accept more than half the responsibility, blame, or guilt for any problem in the relationship, because at her core, she doesn't believe she deserves to be happy." In the bedroom, she will pride herself on her prowess, performing any and all sex acts requested of her. She'll live for thrilling her man and will believe that if she masters the art of lovemaking she will keep his interest. She will also make the fatal mistake of confusing love with sex, causing her to long for it as much as a relationship, just for the "feeling" of being loved that sex gives her. Norwood shares this example of one of her patients who was involved with a married man: "His rapture spurred her on. There was no greater aphrodisiac for her than being able to arouse this man. She responded

powerfully to *his* attraction to *her*. It wasn't her sexuality she was expressing as much as her feelings of being validated by his sexual responsive-
ness to her." Not only do these women confuse sex with love, they also
believe that they can make someone love them. It never works, but it
keeps them focused on conquering a man with sex rather than achieving any kind of emotional intimacy.

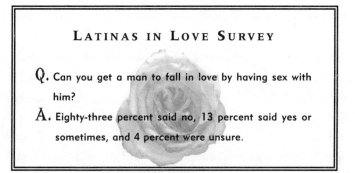

LATINAS IN LOVE SURVEY

Q. Can you get a man to fall in love by having sex with
him?

A. Eighty-three percent said no, 13 percent said yes or
sometimes, and 4 percent were unsure.

What is there for a man to object to, you might ask? The downside
from a man's perspective is that a Latina who loves too much is also
emotionally needy and manipulative. These women frighten easily and
will need constant reassurance that they're loved. Ironically, even
though they believe that they perform well under pressure, they're not
so tough; in fact, they're high maintenance. A woman who loves too
much may suffer for her man, but she won't do it quietly. She'll deploy
guilt bombs on a regular basis to remind him of all she's done for him.
Also, because she uses sex to manipulate rather than express love, a
common complaint will be, "How can the sex be so good but the
relationship so rotten?" Although these women are insecure and want

nurturing, they would be shocked to know that like men, they manage to disconnect emotionally during sex. Instead, they focus entirely on pleasuring their partner, which means, they'll try anything. Technically, they may be experts in the sack, but because they miss out on the emotional bonding that making love can produce, the act tends to become deliberate and automatic. These are also the women who make the classic mistake of thinking they can change a man. This is what motivates them to date "losers" because they want to create the type of ideal family life that they missed. The possibility that they might be able to right past wrongs, to gain something they have lost or never had is what convinces these women they are in love. Much like the fairy tale of *Beauty and the Beast*, women who love too much believe that their love can change a man from the beast he appears to be on the outside into the hero that's hiding inside of him. Not only is the effort futile, it also places the fate of her happiness in someone else's hands. What if he doesn't change? Trust Pilar on this one: Odds are he won't. Considering the unpredictability of human nature, this is a risky venture, but it also allows women who love too much to shuck the responsibility of creating their own happiness and addressing the problems in the relationship.

Bad Habits May Die Hard, but They Will Die

IN ALL MY experiences as a friend and a columnist, this ill-conceived approach by women to love is the most common and the most difficult to change. I've known so many women who believed that they could maintain relationships with a man by having sex with him, or by loving him selflessly, or who looked to men to validate them. Even if a guy started dating another woman but continued to call, come over, and spend the night with a Latina who loved too much, she would be convinced that she was his true love and that one day he would "come to his senses." Some women continually suppress their needs or desires in order to please their men, to the point where they give up their individual identity to become one half of a couple. When that happens, the relationship is doomed because her needs won't be met and the feelings of deprivation, especially when she's doing all she can to keep him happy, will eventually surface. No matter what, a couple is always going to be two individuals coming together as partners. The outmoded, over-romanticized concept that a couple melds together to form a whole places them in a precarious position. Since neither one is truly aware but operating simply on faith, one false move can wreck the relationship's equilibrium. Women who love too much are created early in life when they learn to sacrifice themselves for the greater good of the family. Unlearning that lesson involves rediscovering your identity and embracing it.

For women who love too much, the future isn't entirely bleak. The first step, however is to learn to recognize the signs. To do that, you have to be completely honest with yourself about how you feel. Ask yourself if you're happy and if the answer is no, then ask yourself why. This will require a Latina who loves too much to identify and then curb two of her most often-used survival tools: denial and control. How many Latinas do you know who deny their own feelings and seem happiest only when doing things for others—planning the activities of another adult's life as if he is a child incapable of acting for himself?

Another indicator is the tendency to bury your emotions. We use denial and control to protect ourselves, but this lack of vulnerability will also keep you from letting go, trusting, and sharing real emotional intimacy with your partner. If you ignore your own feelings, your judgment becomes impaired, and that's why men who should be avoided come into your life.

Too often, women who love too much will have sought advice from family members and friends but then ignored this advice. In order to identify the root of her problems, one way a woman who loves too much can try to clear her head is to think back on all that advice. Weren't her friends telling her that the guy was a loser, that he didn't appreciate her, or that he didn't deserve her? These are people who truly love her and who tried to provide positive reinforcement, but she chose to trust and believe in a man who mistreated her, made her feel bad about herself

A woman who loves too much has to exchange this kind of martyrdom for some selfishness. I always tell women who are having difficulty moving on from a failed relationship that the best way to get over it is to pamper themselves. By doing so, they focus on making themselves happy, and although it's not a cure for a broken heart, it is a step in the right direction because each moment spent not thinking about the man or the failed relationship is progress in the right direction. For women who love too much, the concept of being selfish is completely foreign. They've spent their lives sacrificing, struggling, and searching for ways to satisfy their partner, deliberately oblivious to their own needs and pain. But to enjoy a healthy relationship, a woman has to be in tune with herself. She has to know herself, what she wants in a relationship, and what she needs to be happy.

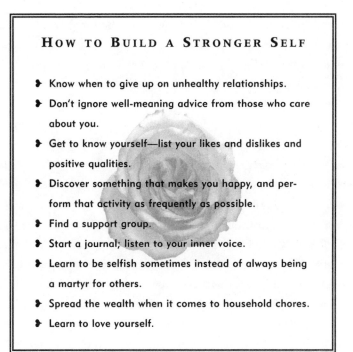

HOW TO BUILD A STRONGER SELF

- ❧ Know when to give up on unhealthy relationships.
- ❧ Don't ignore well-meaning advice from those who care about you.
- ❧ Get to know yourself—list your likes and dislikes and positive qualities.
- ❧ Discover something that makes you happy, and perform that activity as frequently as possible.
- ❧ Find a support group.
- ❧ Start a journal; listen to your inner voice.
- ❧ Learn to be selfish sometimes instead of always being a martyr for others.
- ❧ Spread the wealth when it comes to household chores.
- ❧ Learn to love yourself.

The next step is to take action by changing your behavior to reflect your commitment to building a stronger self. For women who love too much with families, start forcing the kids to do chores rather than taking them all on. Make time to have lunch with a friend or go shopping—for new shoes or antiques, not groceries or clothes for *tu esposa*.

For single women, think of all the signs you ignored, the times when you knew this guy was a loser and you talked yourself into giving him another chance. The inner voice inside us all is our best defender and protector because it's never wrong. Women who love too much learn to shut it out, but once they accept that self-preservation isn't a weakness, that voice will get louder and stronger. To heed your inner voice regarding what is healthy for you, and then follow its directives, is how you develop a stronger self.

From learning to be a little selfish comes the next, most important step, which is learning to love yourself. That is really the key to the universe when it comes to healthy relationships. Women who love too much are selfless, and although in some situations it's considered noble, to be selfless twenty-four hours a day, seven days a week is to be a nonperson, unworthy of any notice or care, a.k.a. a doormat. Loving yourself tells the world, "I am someone, I am worthy, and if you don't agree, piss off!" To Latinas, this sounds unladylike, but remember, it's an inner voice. You won't be wearing a placard with the words printed on it, but the thought will cross your mind, especially when you feel you're being treated in a less than worthy manner. Self-love means you can look in the mirror and believe that you wouldn't want to be anyone else. You feel comfortable in your own skin and are not concerned with pleasing or entertaining anyone to get them to like you. You like your life and who you are, and even if someone else is prettier, or smarter, or richer, damn it, your life is good. Only after a woman can accept and love herself will she be cured of loving too much.

8

The Love Life of Mature Latinas

Older Latinas Embrace Modern Ideas for Romance.

Querida Pilar,

I've been divorced for fifteen years. I have two children, but they're both out of the house. I've dated off and on over the past fifteen years, but lately I've noticed a trend. The men who ask me out are getting younger and younger. It's very flattering, but the problem is, I would like to meet a man my age or older. What should I do?

Marta, 45

WHEN IT COMES to love, the best cure for bad habits is age. Like all women, as Latinas get older, they also get wiser. The different factors in life that affect our relationships—whether it's the influence of our mothers, how "Americanized" we are, if we're a Latina who loves too much, or if we're a member of Generations X, Y, and Ñ—don't really matter as much when we're experienced. For most women over forty, the compelling questions have been answered, the problems solved, and the mistakes corrected. These women either never married, or got married but became widowed or divorced, like our dear pal Marta. As they reach their forties and fifties, they are accomplished, independent, and self-confident Latinas. Those who never married may feel antsy about being single, but they also know that if that never happens, they'll be okay. They have a job that they love, and if not, they can at least support themselves, enjoy their freedom, and enjoy all the things that makes their quality of life pretty damn good.

For Latinas reentering the dating arena after a marriage breakup or loss of a loved one, the prospect does not seem enticing. They're not likely to panic because they can support themselves and they may focus initially on self-improvement or better yet, pampering. They may opt out of the dating scene and go it alone for a while, choosing to look inward rather than outward for companionship. Indeed, the best companion for a woman after a breakup is herself. There is a popular misconception that a woman needs to have a man in her life or that women are relationship obsessed, but from what I've observed, more men than women "relationship hop." But no matter how much self-exploration she does, a woman does get lonely, and although the thought of dating may be a little scary "at her age," she will eventually venture out. Studies show that men and women live longer if they have a partner as they age. I'm not saying that women need men in their lives, but if a Latina happens upon one, especially as she gets older, it never hurts to hook up.

Still Dating After All These Years

WHEN IT COMES to dating over forty, there are two scenarios for Latinas: they either never married or they've been married and find themselves single again. For the former, obviously the idea is to find Mr. Right, but as yet he hasn't been spotted. These women have kissed a lot of frogs but so far, no prince. Some may, however, look back on one former love who, in retrospect, might be the one who got away. Women at this age will begin to doubt their methods. While they may consider being single a lifestyle choice, deep down inside they admit that finding a life partner would be nice.

Never fear, ladies. In romance, there's one rule that can help cure those bittersweet memories: coulda, shoulda, woulda. He could have been right for you but if he had, you should have known, and if you had known, you would have married him. It really is that simple. I have a few of those in my own history, but if I look at the ones who got away, honestly, I know it never would have worked. One particular "what if" suffered from a madonna/whore complex, or more simply, he wanted to marry a nice girl and have her bear his children, but he wanted to have sex with a bad girl. In his mind, his wife and his lover had to be two completely different people. So when I ask myself, "What if I had married him?" the answer is, he would have cheated on me.

Single, mature Latinas have a lot going for them. They're strong, independent, intelligent, educated, self-sufficient, attractive, and self-confident. They've read all the women's magazines to learn about what to wear on a date—some may even have tried Helen Gurley Brown's ill-conceived suggestion of putting on wet panties so that your dress will stick to them—and they've taken the *Cosmo* sex quiz to rate themselves as lovers. They've joined health clubs and bought the latest skin care products to give them that healthy youthful glow. Latinas forty and over are fully developed professionally, physically, mentally, and spiritually. They may wonder why they haven't met someone with whom they can have a long-term relationship or, in the words of singer Paula Cole, "Where have all the cowboys gone?" A strong, confident woman who is not codependent or needy is not going to be compatible with just anyone. She'll have to find a guy with the same attributes. The Latina over forty will need a bit of luck finding him, so it wouldn't hurt to light a candle, rub Buddha's belly, or invest in a rabbit's foot. If these methods fail, it may indeed be time to reassess the situation, including her methods and even expectations.

LATINAS IN LOVE SURVEY

Among women responding to the survey, the highest-income Latinas were the oldest. The average salary for respondents over forty was $60,000.

Reassessing doesn't necessarily require change. It can also reaffirm that you're on the right track. I knew a career-minded Latina in Texas who was determined to marry. Since she had no interest in having children, the urgency did not escalate until she turned forty. She had had a few long-term relationships, but still hadn't met Mr. Right. After the age of thirty-five, she gave each beau a year to propose, and if he didn't, she dumped him instantly. She figured that she didn't have the time to waste on a man who wasn't interested in marrying. She was incredibly confident and quite capable of supporting herself but hated the prospect of being labeled a "spinster." After a couple of years of this, she decided to reassess. She began to think that her standards were too high and that maybe she had passed on guys who could have made her happy. She concluded that this, combined with the extreme approach of setting a deadline for a commitment, had doomed her to failure. Without knowing it, each man was on a very short leash time-wise, and preoccupied with getting that ring and settling down, she never really took the time to know these men either, which is why they were easily replaced. She did marry eventually, but not until she was well into her forties and to a man who was well below her original "standards." She ran out of time and had to choose a man who was not the physical image of her ideal guy, but who was kind and treated her well. In this case, it certainly looks like she "settled," and I would never encourage anyone to do that. Any man is *not* better than no man; in fact, alone is really better than *any* man. In the end, however, I don't think she settled. She did get what she wanted; she was no longer a spinster.

Her experience begs the question: Is it possible to be too confident? Women do need to know who they are and what they want, but they also have to understand that a relationship takes two people working together to make it a success. Normally the "my way or the highway" attitude should work in weeding out the less viable males, but as we get older and men continue to chose the highway, it might be time to think about what went wrong. Focused on getting what they want, some women may be so adept at identifying their own needs that they become a little inflexible when it comes to anyone else's. Believe it or not, guys have feelings too! They also have egos, and they're not going to choose a woman who makes them feel inadequate, just as a woman will not choose a man who makes her feel like she should lose a few pounds.

A relationship is a give-and-take situation. When you care about someone, you want to make him happy and if your partner feels the same way about you, then he'll tend to your needs. When it works, neither one notices, but when it doesn't, when the give and take gets out of balance, he or she will quickly begin to tally who does what for whom and how often. If you're over forty and still single and your relationships aren't working, it may be time to consider what you bring to a relationship, the good and the bad. Are you uncompromising? Do you expect to get your way all the time? Are you high-maintenance? Are your expectations about romance realistic? If you have a man in your life who loves and respects you, and you can see yourself living with him for the rest of your life, then you have to work at it. Unromantic as it sounds, after the first few months of a relationship, or the isn't-it-great-we-both-like-Chinese-food stage, as Mary Richards on *The Mary Tyler Moore Show* put it, relationships aren't easy, they're hard work.

FORTY-PLUS LATINA ROLE MODELS

- ❧ Cristina Saralegui—media mogul
- ❧ Rita Moreno—entertainer, actress
- ❧ Ileana Ros-Lehtinen—congresswoman
- ❧ Linda Alvarado—entrepreneur
- ❧ Linda Chavez-Thompson—labor leader
- ❧ Celia Cruz—singer

Adding to the stress of dating after forty are the forces of nature. For an older woman who has never been married and who wants a child, the old biological clock is no longer ticking. The alarm has gone off and the snooze button is broken. Despite the plethora of celebrities having children over forty, medical research confirms that a woman's chances of getting pregnant after the age of thirty-five are greatly reduced, and the caliber of her eggs also declines, as does a man's sperm after the same age. In this situation, it can be a drag being a girl, especially if you want a child and there's no man around. There are solutions to this problem, like artificial insemination or adoption, but for women who just want to settle down, the problem is not so easily solved. A good man is sometimes hard to find, especially if they're only interested in finding twenty-something wives. She may have assumed that the man she's looking for is older and richer, but with Generation X so eager to be adult, and many making their first million or two before they hit thirty, it may behoove her to check out those "tenderonies" (men ten or more years younger). In many cases, the battle may be half won since these young men seem to appreciate mature women.

LATINAS IN LOVE SURVEY

Q. What age do you prefer in a mate?

A. Forty-eight percent said they prefer an older mate (five to ten years), 35 percent preferred a mate the same age, 11 percent chose a younger male (five to ten years), 4 percent had no preference, and 2 percent preferred much older men (more than ten years).

Youthful Pleasures

MORE THAN ONE Latina over forty has complained to me that she only gets asked out by younger guys. While it's flattering, these Latinas would prefer to date someone their own age or older. "Younger men aren't mature, and I don't want to be anyone's mommy," offered one. It's not surprising that younger men are attracted to older Latinas. Compared to women their own age, older women offer these men a fairly straightforward relationship. It begins with companionship and may or may not turn into a committed relationship. Remember, this is the generation (X, Ñ) that appreciates honesty above all else. This is also a generation that wants to grow up fast, and what better way to enter the world of real adults than by dating one. Older Latinas don't feel that they have to prove anything. They're comfortable in their own skins, which means they're less likely to play games or use tricks to get a man. If they've been married, they're also not in a rush to settle down. They can take their time and allow themselves to be entertained.

Younger men do provide challenges, but they also offer advantages. To begin with, they have stamina. For women who have found passion lacking in older men, younger men will more than make up for it. It's true that men mature more slowly than women, but sexually, a younger man and older woman are actually more compatible since women reach their sexual peak in their late thirties, early forties and men reach their sexual peak in their late teens, early twenties. Younger men find an older woman's experience and maturity genuinely appealing. For many women, being desired is an aphrodisiac. Someone you may not think fits your idea of the ultimate dude can give you a look that makes you say, "Hmmmm, he's kinda cute." When a man finds you attractive, though you shouldn't value yourself based on that, it's still very seductive. Regardless of her accomplishments or her bankroll, a woman needs to be desired. When that person is a successful, strapping younger man, what's there to complain about?

Well, the biggest obstacle to this kind of union is social pressure. Men who snag younger wives have always been applauded, but when women date younger men they're accused of "robbing the cradle." In *The Graduate*, Mrs. Robinson was portrayed as a desperate, unscrupulous woman, grasping at youth by taking the son of her best friends as a lover. In 1998, Terry McMillan's bestseller *How Stella Got Her Groove Back* turned a social taboo into a viable option for older women. In 2002, the film *Tadpole* tackled the subject yet again and spawned a new term, "tadpoling," to describe the younger-man-older-woman romance.

You say you don't feel comfortable dating a guy who looks like he's young enough to be your son? That may seem like a drag, but you have to remember that these guys don't see it that way. They want to be with an older woman because they are more attracted to them than to girls their own age. Most Latinas look younger than their real age anyway, and maintaining a youthful look simply requires the proper diet (drink lots of water), exercise, hygiene, and most importantly, attitude. Many Hollywood couples, like Susan Sarandon and Tim Robbins (twelve-year gap), Juliet Mills and Maxwell Caufield (eighteen years), Ralph Fiennes and Francesca Annis (nineteen years), and Raquel Welch and Richard Palmer (fourteen years), provide examples of how older women and younger men can be successful in love. These women, and many others who are not famous and who've tried it, are not complaining. In *Older Women, Younger Men: New Options for Love and Romance*, authors Felicia Brings and Susan Winter interviewed two hundred "tadpolers" about their relationships. From their interviews, they dispelled three myths about younger-men-older-women couples: the relationships do last, they're not just about sex, and the younger men do not dump their older wives for younger women. According to the latest Census, 12 percent of married couples and 21 percent of unwed couples living together involve an older woman and a younger man.

SKY HIGH EXPECTATIONS

Are you holding out for the impossible? Look at your expectations when it comes to finding a man—Do you consider yourself high-maintenance? Do you always need to have things your way? Take some time to examine your standards and see if any of them need changing.

Whether or not she has a man in her life, a Latina in her forties is embarking on one of the most important chapters of her existence. Many forty-year-olds I've known have expressed a sense of freedom and liberation about turning forty. "Your life is finally your own at this age," said one. She has complete and total control of her life and with that, the power to do whatever she wants. She can travel, she can go back to school, she can take skydiving lessons, or she can just stay home and read. The more urgent she is about finding a man, the more prone she will be to making a mistake. Once a woman accepts that she can live alone for the rest of her life and be just fine, the rest is easy.

There's an old adage that says you find love when you're least expecting it, and as adages go, this one is pretty accurate. We know that the best way to meet someone is through friends or by joining a club or group that shares your interests. Bars and office dating are considered taboo, but single professional women tend to socialize the most in these settings. The odds against meeting someone at this stage in life do seem stacked against them, which only adds to their sense of urgency, and the only way to be free of it is to abandon the search. Don't worry about it anymore, leave it up to fate, and concentrate on living life to the fullest. Stay active, don't shut yourself off from people, and take each day one day at a time.

Amor, the Second (or Third) Time Around

FOR WOMEN IN their forties or fifties who have been married and are entering the dating scene after a divorce, it's all good. There's no anxiety about getting married; been there, done that. There's usually no biological clock ticking because the babies have been made. Once again, this woman is independent and self-sufficient. Her ego may be a bit bruised, however, because there's no rejection more harsh than that of divorce. Once the deed is done, divorced women need to take time for introspection. Many will fret over past mistakes, like choosing their ex-husband in the first place, or staying with him for so long. This is normal, but women should be careful not to let it last too long, no more than a few months. This kind of thinking is futile—you can't change the past so there's no sense regretting it.

Past mistakes serve to teach us a lesson, so during this time of reflection, it's important to identify what went wrong and why. It's also important to try and move past the anger, and while that may be difficult at first, it helps to concentrate on the positive results from the relationship. Something good had to have come out of the marriage, like finishing a college degree or having children. Once you find that positive thing, or things, it's time to move forward and start looking toward the future, which is wide open. Someone once told me that turning forty was very empowering because it meant that you were finally a real adult. Reentering the dating game at this age, and with so much more life experience than a person in her twenties is certainly empowering.

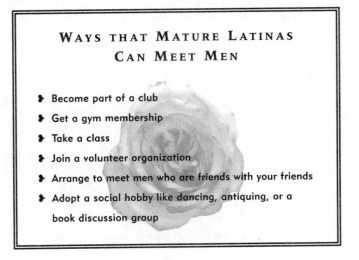

WAYS THAT MATURE LATINAS CAN MEET MEN

- ❧ Become part of a club
- ❧ Get a gym membership
- ❧ Take a class
- ❧ Join a volunteer organization
- ❧ Arrange to meet men who are friends with your friends
- ❧ Adopt a social hobby like dancing, antiquing, or a book discussion group

If you are in this situation, this is the time to take stock of all the dreams and ambitions that got cast aside, one by one, while you focused on your marriage. Marriage means compromises and missed opportunities, which may include your childhood aspirations. With the single life comes the freedom to be selfish. Moms will still have to care for the kids but by this time, they may be older and beginning to branch out on their own. As Latinas, we learn that selfishness is never a good thing, so it will take practice to start doing things just for yourself.

A facial is always a nice way to get the ball rolling. It's expensive and therefore decadent, but because of the way it makes you feel, not to mention the way it benefits your skin, it's also worth it. One woman I know was married to an asthmatic man. Once they divorced, she got two dogs, not out of spite, but because she loves dogs and could never have them in the house. She also bought wonderful scented candles, not just to cover up the house's newfound doggy odor, but because she could never have them before. It's those simple things that get us through a crisis, and after divorce, your first objective should be to pamper yourself, on a small and large scale.

LATINAS IN LOVE SURVEY

Q. What is the most important thing you learned from your marriage?

A. Several of the women surveyed who were divorced or married more than once said that the most important thing that they learned was to respect themselves and to have open communication.

When it comes to dating for mature Latinas, the best part is the lack of urgency. A woman who has been married can afford to be picky. She knows what she wants and doesn't want and since she's just learning to enjoy being alone in her house, she may not be in a hurry to find a new relationship. She can enjoy the "tenderonies" who will undoubtedly come her way, or just stay at home and take a nice long bubble bath. She can plan an adventure, go on a trip, or trek back to school to finish the degree that she gave up to get married. Honestly, finding a man will probably be at the bottom of the list of must-dos for these women, but having an occasional companion to the movies, a play, or the opera is nice. Because this is a time to explore and blossom as a new woman, it may also be time to get involved in a cause. Women at this stage have the time and the much needed expertise to help out a nonprofit organization. It's also a great way to meet guys, not that it should be the objective, but it beats a bar or church.

Some are also single mothers who held off entering into a serious relationship until after their children were grown and are now ready to fall in love. These women have earned their independence and are not in a hurry to give it up. For women who do have children still living at home but don't want to wait, I suggest that they practice some discretion when dating. Definitely don't bring the man home to stay overnight unless the relationship takes a serious turn, and even then, I suggest you wait until you remarry. Kids will have a tough enough time getting used to a new man in their lives, but it's even more difficult if they happen to grow attached to a man only to lose him when your relationship ends and he doesn't come around anymore. I know of one example where a recently divorced woman went on a man-hunt, dating and sleeping with as many men as possible. She had a young daughter at home whom she neglected in order to date. She had a real need to express her newfound freedom and sexuality. Her daughter, however, learned that she could not depend on her mother. She became insecure and, like her mother, dependent on a man for her sense of security. She got married just shy of her seventeenth birthday.

A lot can happen to divorced women in their forties and fifties. In some cases, old romances are rekindled, though as we get older, the prospect of attending a high school reunion gets less and less appealing. Without a six-figure income, a husband to show off, or a miraculously maintained high school figure, many of us don't eagerly anticipate showing up to the event a little wiser and a lot older. We forget, however, that the people in that room have also aged. I've noticed that it's hard for me to tell if the people closest to me have aged, so when I run into an old friend, many times I think she looks the same. Except for the few *viejos* who still consider themselves players and are still trying to bag those young things, chances are your old boyfriend will see you in the same flattering light.

The best news about dating over forty is these Latinas can take it or leave it. Sure, a relationship would be nice, but they know how to live alone, they know they can survive on their own and be happy, and rather than trade in their independence for codependence, they are willing to wait. The options are wide open for divorced or widowed women in their forties and fifties. They've got nothing to prove and a long time to enjoy things. They know exactly what they want, and that kind of confidence is a luxury. Mature Latinas are picky and proud of it.

9

Learning to Listen

Our Inner Voice is Never Wrong, and Men Mean What They Say

Dear Amiga Mía,

I have been seeing this guy for the past six months. We began as friends and then it became romantic. The romantic part has been the six months. Our relationship has been physically intimate the whole time. After our first night together, he told me that he cared about me, but that he was not looking for a serious relationship. Six months later, he's still saying the same thing. Am I fooling myself or will he ever fall in love with me? I, of course, fell in love six months ago. He's everything I ever wanted in a man.

Petra, 26

'M CONCERNED ABOUT what has happened to Petra. She isn't listening to what her boyfriend is saying. She's also ignoring whatever her inner voice is saying. Why? Because hope springs eternal.

Many theories thrive about the differences between women and men. One says that we're made of sugar and spice and everything nice and that they're made of snakes and snails and puppy dog tails. Another theory claims we hail from Venus and they come from Mars. The brutally honest Dr. Phil McGraw asserts that men and women are wired differently. The bottom line is that men and women are different. When it comes to romance, men and women approach love in their own distinct ways. Generally, men are motivated by sex; women are motivated by fantasy. There are challenges when the two get together, but there is also great fun.

Rather than trying to conquer these differences, men and women should embrace them, and in this way, learn to understand each other. Many men prefer to use the "ignorance is bliss" excuse and give up trying to understand women. They seem to accept the universal truth that occasionally women do need to feel like goddesses. Women, however, seem to find challenges, especially in men, irresistible. As nurturers and caregivers, we think we can love a man enough to change him, or as we prefer to see it, bring out the best in him. Rather than see the men in our lives for who they are, we see who they could become, and often fall in love with hopes and dreams rather than flesh and bone.

As an advice columnist, one of the most common letters I receive concerns the struggle to accept the truth, as Petra's letter demonstrates. Once women become emotionally attached to an idea, especially one they've created, it's almost impossible to let it go. In their letters, these women are confused because they see their boyfriends "acting" a certain way, but then when pressed to express their feelings, they "say" something completely different. Many women will ignore the signs that a relationship isn't working and coach themselves into believing that all will be well. The main technique they use is to mentally contradict what their partner may be telling them. Rather than accept the truth, a woman assumes that her man doesn't know what he's talking about and that, in time, he will "see the light." Some women create a vision of the future that ends happily ever after, so abandoning the dream in order to accept the truth is not a viable option. Denial is not just a river in Egypt, which makes breaking up even harder to do.

There is one important tool for self-preservation, especially in love, that women forget to use. That tool is the little inner voice. Because the voice is usually subconscious, listening to it takes practice. And while a Latina needs to learn how to hear to her own inner voice, I also advise her to listen to what her man is saying. Invariably, he's telling the truth.

The Little Inner Voice

WE KNOW IT when we hear it. It's that subconscious shout that says, 'Stop! Wait! Think!" When you're in tune with it, it can be so palpable at times that it causes a physical pause; we literally stop in our tracks. For example, say one morning you decide you'd like a warm breakfast, and so breakfast tacos are on the menu. You turn on the burner to warm the *comál* to warm the tortillas. You're about to reach across the stove to grab the *comál* and put it on the burner, but for some reason, you pause. You're wearing a robe with long, loose, low hanging sleeves. Without thinking, you stop, just in time to notice how close your flammable garment is to the flames. The little voice let out a shout, you listened, and a potential household accident was avoided. If you really listen, the little voice can be a great help in romance too. Love can come down to a matter of survival, but when it's the psyche and not the body that's in danger, the little voice has to make itself heard above the din of our insecurities. When it works, or if we're feeling particularly confident that day, we hear it and pay attention. But on a bad day, when chocolate is our best and only friend, the little voice will turn to physical disruption, such as a stomachache, in order to be heard.

In love, we become our own psychic, psychologist, and spiritualist. We constantly talk to ourselves trying to assess the situation and our own feelings. "What sign is he?" "Does he like me?" "Am I too fat?" "Was I a good lover?" "Does he love me?" "Is he ready to make a commitment?" "Gee, I'd love to get married and bear his children!" All these thoughts spin around and around in our heads. Some begin after the first date, others crop up as the relationship progresses and don't stop until he says, "I do." Of course these are just a few internal questions; many more will certainly emerge, and remain constant. The little voice, normally so subconscious that we just automatically do what it tells us to do rather than wait to hear it, has to shout past the racket. Miraculously, it does. Sometimes we listen, but usually we're preoccupied.

The great thing about the little voice is that it's got enormous power and tenacity. It never gives up. It can make us feel queasy, anxious, and unsettled. It'll make us cry if it has to, just to get our attention, but the little voice knows it has to be cruel to be kind. It's our little voice and it loves us. It just wants the best for us, and it will do what it has to do to protect us and steer us in the right direction.

Think of your little voice as your own personal Pilar. It wants what is best for you.

SIGNS THAT YOUR LITTLE VOICE IS BEING IGNORED

- You get queasy when you think about the guy you're dating
- You try to get everyone's take on what he says and what he does to make you feel better
- You start to talk yourself into doing things you know you shouldn't, sometimes out loud
- You cry yourself to sleep because he hasn't called you
- You start every conversation with, "Do you think he likes me?"
- You like it when friends tell you what you want to hear and stop speaking to them when they don't

My mother gave me great advice, and for this reason, I was known to quote the adage, "Your mother's always right," to many friends as they struggled with boy trouble during high school. I accepted these as words of wisdom, assuming that if young women listened to their moms, they could avoid boy trouble. Eventually, I realized that not all women had a mom like mine. Other moms didn't always give the best advice; in fact, many may have made matters worse. I was convinced that there had to be some way that women could stop making the same mistakes in relationships and avoid the usual pitfalls. That's when the little voice spoke up. "What about me?" it asked. "I've never steered you wrong." It was true. I dated a lot in college and looking back, I can say with a minimum of heartache. With each boyfriend, I learned something about myself and what I expected from a guy, especially how I wanted to be treated.

Women have been called great manipulators, but guys are just as expert at it. One trick they use is feigned indifference. Comments like, "I'll call you sometime" or not calling after a date for several days are little manipulations. These tactics get a girl's insecurities going and prompt her to ask questions like, "Does he like me?" until she can't rest until she hears from him again. One boyfriend, a Latino business student, was the sweetest, cutest, nicest guy, but he had a friend who was quite the cad. I never understood the friendship, since the two guys were so different, but I realize now that it makes sense, à la Dean Moriarty and Sal Paradise in Jack Kerouac's *On the Road*. Many mild mannered guys have studly womanizers as friends, whom they seem to admire and envy. Dave and I dated over the summer. His friend spent the summer in his hometown. Everything was swell until the fall, when the friend returned. Suddenly, this sweet, nice guy started to swagger and his conversation got more and more vague. We had gone out regularly over the summer, but when school started, I barely saw him or heard from him. On our last date, he uttered those stupid words, "I'll call you sometime." The little voice in me shouted, "As if," (this was during the eighties, okay?) and I never went out with him again. I think he was shocked at how quickly I could turn on my heel and never see him again. I don't think it was in his nature to be a cad, really, but I wasn't going to give him a chance to try it on me. I had dated enough guys to spot manipulation when it happened, and I refused to put up with it.

WHERE IS YOUR LITTLE INNER VOICE?

Think back to a time when you got that strange gut feeling that something wasn't quite right when you were out on a date. Or how you felt that moment your date did or said something that you didn't like. Remember that moment—that was your little inner voice chiming in to give you advice and guidance.

My little inner voice was obviously quite strong, but I wondered why more women couldn't hear theirs. We all hear something, but at a certain stage in all our lives we reach a fork in the road and opt to develop our inner voice or squelch it. The little inner voice has an enabler called self-confidence. Without it, many women can't or won't be warned. This is where moms are critical. They can teach their daughters to demand respect from men, or they can teach them to be the doormat in a relationship. Unfortunately, not all moms get the right job done, but the little inner voice is never completely destroyed. A girl will still be bothered when a guy says he'll call her and doesn't or when he tells her he just wants to be friends after a night of passionate sex. That inner voice is not a gift; it's an instinct. Even women with the lowest self-esteem have a little inner voice. Many abused women, for example, will eventually seek help, so clearly, it's there. It's meant to help us so it makes sense to take that voice seriously because it's always right.

Learning to listen can be a real challenge. If you're out of practice, start with the phone call test. If a guy doesn't call after the first date, that's a red flag, which is what the little voice warns you about. It puts out red flags to make you stop, wait, and think about any behavior that is potentially harmful. The first red flag doesn't necessarily mean that you should drop the guy, although it might not be a bad idea. But it does mean, "Pay attention!" If you do go out with him again, you should definitely be on your guard. As the relationship progresses, be mindful of any actions or words that lack respect. If by this time you're too enthralled to listen, you'll know if something's wrong by that uneasy feeling you get when a guy doesn't open the door, or walks ten paces ahead, or spends the entire night talking about how much he loves to work out.

The down side of the little voice is that since its purpose is to raise red flags, the news isn't usually good. That's why it makes you feel queasy and uneasy rather than nervously excited. It may seem louder in the early stages of a relationship because you're not so inundated by other mental noise, which makes this the best and easiest time to walk away from a bad relationship—better a little hurt now than a lot of hurt later.

LATINAS IN LOVE SURVEY

Q. Should women should assume that most men are: "dogs," "human beings," or "they shouldn't assume?"

A. Sixty-four percent said that "they shouldn't assume"; 24 percent chose "human beings"; and 11 percent of the Latinas surveyed chose "dogs."

A question on the survey about whether Latinas view men as "dogs" or human beings was meant to discover how cynical Latinas have become toward men. One of the few Latinas who assume men are dogs wrote: "I know this sounds immature, but I think that if a woman uses this as a defense mechanism she can save face if needed, *but*, she needs to understand that men *are* human beings." I assumed that many more would choose "dogs" as an answer, but clearly, Latinas remain very open-minded and little naive (and therefore vulnerable) where men are concerned. It behooves us to learn from past mistakes and to take note of bad behavior.

For those who weren't paying attention, here's another tip. Manipulation is a sign of insecurity as well as immaturity. Besides not calling after the first date, another little psychological trick guys use is to transfer their own insecurities onto the girl. As soon as he starts to criticize you, you should know that he's trying to make you feel insecure so that you'll feel lucky to have him. It's a backwards compliment; obviously he doesn't feel worthy to have you, but the intent is insidious. The criticisms usually involve trying to make you "a better person," so at first it seems like he cares. If a guy's smart, he'll never mention weight loss, but he will mention things like lack of ambition or lack of self-discipline, under the guise of promoting your own self-improvement. As a columnist, this is one of the most common complaints I receive from women—husbands or boyfriends who constantly criticize. If you don't have a strong sense of self, this type of manipulation can be very effective. Perhaps not calling after the first date or criticism aren't your big issues, but whenever a guy does cross the line, the little inner voice will raise a red flag inside you by giving you a kick in the belly. When you get that feeling, recognize that it's your little inner voice telling you, "Stop, wait, and think! This person is not treating you with respect or love. Is this really the guy for you? You deserve better. You are worth more than this."

Men Mean What They Say, Women Watch What They Do

AS LITTLE GIRLS, we are told that actions speak louder than words. Perhaps this comment was meant to discourage us from making empty promises or to relieve parents from offering constant verbal reassurances to their children—Daddy and Mommy love you because they work hard and buy you candy, clothes, and cars. Whatever the reason, this advice only encouraged our intuitiveness. We grew up thinking that our objective was to get past the verbal façade and to the heart of the matter by reading body language and interpreting it.

Sometimes the advice works; sometimes it doesn't. Facial expressions can reveal an honest emotion well before the brain has a chance to smother it. Criminal investigators, from the sheriff to the Federal Bureau of Investigation, study body language for any signs that contradict a verbal statement. For example, nose rubbing or any hand-to-face movements have proven to be spontaneous responses that expose an uncomfortable subconscious. A hand-to-the-heart motion, on the other hand, is considered a genuinely sincere gesture. It's understandable that some women are misled into applying the same theory to romance. Touching, like holding hands or placing a hand on the waist or shoulder, is one way couples express tenderness, especially if it happens spontaneously. It the contact is overdone or required on demand, however, one wonders if a couple doth protest too much. Certain gestures too can be romantic, such as flowers (just because and not as an apology), or surprise gifts, like a massage or an engagement ring. Whether by tradition or nature, these signs are accepted ways that men show their desire and attraction to a woman. As the relationship progresses, they signal a man's continued love and affection for his mate.

Men do show their love through these gestures and they do help reinforce a man's true feelings, but to do this, these actions must happen in good times, not bad. When the relationship is in trouble, gestures like these can be confusing and act only as a temporary solution to a bigger problem. When problems arise, the woman's little voice will start to nag, but if she's trained herself to ignore it, she's got to learn to listen to what her man's telling her if she's going to spare herself additional distress.

I have a theory that might clear up some of the confusion. As men and women struggle to get along, it strikes me that it might help if both learned to listen to each other. Many times, I believe that men are trying to be honest, albeit in a cowardly way, and if women simply listened to what men are saying, they could save themselves a lot of grief. My theory is that the root cause of confusion between the sexes is that men mean what they say, but women watch how men act. Remember, women are conditioned to think that actions speak louder than words, so if a guy "acts" romantic, but everything he says is unromantic, a girl will believe that the way he acts is the true reflection of how he feels. The reverse, however, is true and I think women already know this—that's why we're so much better at giving advice than taking it. Jane can easily tell her friend Judy that George isn't treating her right, but when Judy returns the favor, Jane doesn't want to hear it. When we're suffering with a romantic fever, we lose all reason, and advice, especially if it's unwelcome, either adds to the confusion or gets ignored. In the Latinas in Love survey, I posed a question that I thought would reveal how women get confused, but the result proved that Latinas know better—they just need to use the same logic on themselves that they give to their friends.

LATINAS IN LOVE SURVEY

Given three options, Latinas were asked to interpret what it meant when a man has sex with a woman but tells her he just wants to be friends. Eighty percent picked "That he just wants to be friends (and have sex)" and 17 percent checked "That he's not ready for a relationship at this time but could be later." Three percent had no answer, but zero chose "That he's really in love but doesn't know it."

Women are coached to read between the lines, but men don't work that way. For most guys, it's all black and white. Except for the occasional cad, most men don't set out to deceive women. Depending on the situation, men assume that their intentions are fairly obvious. For example, if you meet a guy in a bar, it could be implied that sex is a definite possibility, whereas if you meet a guy through a church group, it's safe to assume that he's looking for a permanent relationship. Since women can work great mental magic, they tend to assume that any guy is a potential mate. Whatever flaws he has in person, she can adjust and improve upon in her head. The majority of Latinas surveyed were right when they said they would take at his word the man who said he just wants to be friends. I think men are trying to be honest when they have sex with a woman but tell her they just want to be friends. Many men can separate sex and love, and some do feel an obligation to be forthright about it. A guy thinks that if he's "honest" at the start and tells a woman that he has no romantic or long-term intentions where she's concerned, that he can continue with the sexual relationship guilt-free, because, after all, "she was warned."

Unfortunately, the situation is not so simple. Guys really are taking advantage of the situation and they know it. What usually happens is the girl goes a little crazy and starts to expect that the relationship is progressing beyond a friendship. No matter how many times he says it, as long as he keeps sleeping with her, a girl will assume that since they have connected physically, it's just a matter of time before the emotional factor kicks in. The longer it takes to happen, however, the more neurotic she will become, and that's a sure sign to the male involved that the girl hasn't heard a word he said. Since his senses are still intact, he should be the one to break things off—permanently.

LATINAS IN LOVE SURVEY

Q. Is it possible to have sex with a man and not fall in love?

A. Among survey respondents, 95 percent of Latinas said yes, 4 percent said no, and 2 percent were unsure.

Unfortunately, it's difficult for men to turn down guilt-free sex. To enter into this kind of arrangement with a woman in the first place is not consistent with the behavior of a man with integrity, so good luck hoping he'll call things off. No, women just have to start listening and stop assuming that they know a man's true intentions or feelings. He really is telling you the truth, and even though it may not be what you want to hear, you should know that it's true. Women will delude themselves by thinking that they are liberated and can have sex without feeling attached, but not if they like a guy. Remember the oxytocin? That's the hormone women produce when breastfeeding, in labor, and during an orgasm, that causes them to bond. No matter how casual she tells herself the sex is, after a while, a woman will feel a bond with the guy she's sleeping with. It's kind of like Las Vegas. You want to hit big and move on. The people who lose the most will stay at a slot machine even after it has paid them and, believing that they'll hit the big jackpot, will put all their winnings back into it. Similarly, if a woman thinks she can have casual sex beyond a one-night-stand, she's asking for trouble.

In a relationship, a man chooses his words very carefully, especially if he wants to be "honest." Men and women don't just have problems communicating; they also have different approaches to sex. No matter how liberated women become, sex for most of us remains a very personal and intimate experience. For some women, however, sex and love get misinterpreted, so much so that they will seek out sex in order to feel loved. For men, the opposite is true. Sex and love are very distinct. One is a physical act; the other involves emotion. Since the world of emotions is a scary place for most men, they avoid it, but that doesn't mean they can't enjoy sex. Where sex games are concerned, guys will always hold an advantage. Women many try to use sex as a weapon or as emotional blackmail, but usually it backfires.

It bears repeating: Women must to learn to listen to their inner voice. When they get that queasy feeling, they should know that something's not quite right, and that they need to be on their guard. The inner voice can ensure that a Latina meets the right guy, not just any guy. If she's managed to tune that inner voice out, the next thing she needs to know is that what a man does doesn't always reflect his true feelings; in fact, the two can be completely different. When a man says he's not interested in a serious relationship or that he likes a woman but just as a friend, he means it, regardless of whether they're intimately involved or not. He may genuinely care about the woman, but not enough to commit. Men also need to accept that they do have a responsibility to be honest and respectful and watch what they do. The truth does sometimes hurt, but to the Latina who's honest and true to herself, it can hurt a lot less.

10

Latinas in Love

What are the basic components of a good relationship?

Dear Pilar,

I used to think that my parents had the best relationship. They've been married for nearly thirty years so that must mean they've done something right, right? I've recently gotten engaged, and I've asked my mom to share the secret of her success. What she told me shocked me. She said that no matter what, the marriage should come first and if it means looking the other way in certain circumstances, then so be it. I don't think I can do that, plus I don't want to become a martyr to my marriage. I love my fiancé, and when I make my vows to marry him 'till death do us part,' I intend to try, but things happen, right? I want to believe that our marriage will last forever, but I'm not willing to sacrifice myself or self esteem to make it happen. Is that wrong? What do you think is the secret to a good relationship?

Vanessa, 28

ANESSA IS RIGHT to be confused, receiving the Old World cues from her mother, yet hearing her own inner voice telling her that is not acceptable. Latinas will continue to struggle with the definition of love and reevaluate what makes a good relationship.

When you're in love, you're sure the object of your affection is the key to your future happiness. The world is a better place because he's in it, and as the object of his affection, you're the luckiest girl in the world. If it works, great, but if it doesn't, you're usually dumfounded. Everyone has felt the pain of a broken heart, the downside of love. When it happens, you're sure you'll never fall in love again and that no other person in the world will ever mean so much to you.

Though somewhat of a misnomer, since the sensation is more gut wrenching than a pain in the chest, heartaches do go away. You can't predict when or how it will happen, but one day, you're simply over it. The sky's blue, the birds are chirping, and the air couldn't smell sweeter. You may decide to take a walk in the park, since it's such a fabulous day, and then it happens. You almost get hit by a Frisbee but are saved by the most gorgeous guy and his dog. It may not be love at first sight, but you definitely hope it becomes more than just a chance encounter. In the blink of an eye, you're ready to take the lover's leap of faith.

Falling in love is relatively easy. Making it last is the real challenge.

RULES AND COMPONENTS OF A
GOOD RELATIONSHIP

According to the 2000 Census, in 1997, 2.4 million couples got married and 1.2 million couples got divorced. The U.S. Census Bureau projects that one out of two marriages that take place today will end in divorce. These are not very encouraging statistics, but couples still take the plunge in good faith. Not every marriage will succeed, but sticking to some basic rules and valuing the components of a good relationship can give them all a fighting chance.

• RULE ONE •

Relationships Are Cyclical

MOST RELATIONSHIP EXPERTS caution couples that a relationship is hard work and its success will reflect the amount of work a couple puts into it. Although this advice seems a bit obvious, it bears repeating because many couples enter into marriage with many romantic delusions. They want to believe that the honeymoon is never over, when in fact, it does end, even for those couples that do manage to keep it going longer than most. Love may bring two people together, but the partnership they form to build a long-term relationship is what keeps them together.

Once a couple accepts this fact, they need to realize one more thing. Relationships are not only hard work; they're also cyclical. There will be good and bad times in any relationship, and they seem to come in waves. Each relationship is unique, but I've observed that every five years, couples will be tested. Some challenges will be insurmountable. Infidelity, for example, is very hard to overcome. It destroys one of the basic elements of a strong relationship—trust—and once that's gone it's very hard to get it back. However, other challenges can be worked out; for example, a husband can be trained to leave the toilet seat down. These challenges will test a couple's solidity or the foundation they've built for their relationship through a strong friendship, good communication, passion, and a sense of humor. Breakups happen when couples give up rather than rolling up their sleeves, trying to work things out, seeking professional help if necessary, and most importantly, riding out the bad times.

• RULE TWO •

Friends Make Great Lovers

A SOLID FRIENDSHIP is extremely important in a good relationship because before you can truly love someone, you need to like him. Big things, such as infidelity or bankruptcy can hit a marriage like a hurricane, but the little things, such as nagging, criticizing, and whining, can do the work of termites and eat away at a relationship until it's left bony, brittle, and barely standing. Establishing a friendship first, before leaping into bed, will always be my recommendation.

In 1994, John Gottman, a professor of psychology at the University of Washington in Seattle, released the results of a twenty-year study he conducted on married couples. During that time, he observed more than two thousand couples and looked at how they dealt with conflict. He concluded that the way couples communicate with each other, nonverbally and verbally, could lead them to a marital impasse. According to Gottman, criticism, contempt, defensiveness, and withdrawal can create a downward spiral in a marriage that will lead to divorce. "A small criticism, unheard and ignored, turns into anger and then into contempt. 'You never ask me how my day went' can turn into 'You don't care about me' and then, 'There's something really wrong with you!' Then the other person gets defensive, which can lead to stonewalling and complete withdrawal." Couples that openly expressed their emotions and were basically willing to duke it out stood a better chance of surviving.

Friends know how to fight, but they also know how to make up. Friendships grow over time, after many dates and several lengthy phone conversations. Friendship establishes trust, another important component, as well as lines of communication. In most situations, and in most relationships, when problems arise they can usually be overcome through open and honest discussion. Communication is a skill that improves with practice. For couples, once those lines of communication break down and they stop talking to each other, it's time to consider seeking therapy or counseling.

• RULE THREE •

Sex and Money Can Still Do Damage

SEVERAL FACTORS CAN disrupt a relationship, but the two most common culprits are sex and money. In today's world, it seems like money shouldn't be as much of a problem, since both partners probably work and fewer males are threatened by a wife who earns more than they do. I don't think couples fight over how much money they spend as much as how little time they spend together. A household with two adults that work full time leaves little time for intimacy. Add children to the mix and the situation worsens. This is where couples have to work at the problem and make time for each other rather than hoping that their schedules will miraculously open up. They will eventually, but not until the kids are out of the house, and that's a mighty long time to wait.

If money is still an issue, especially when there are two breadwinners in the house, I have a simple solution—keep your money separate. In the modern age, there's no reason why the "man of the house" should be in charge of all the money. Rather than combining the debt after marriage, I suggest that couples keep their existing credit card bills separate and apply for a new one jointly. They could also open a joint bank account for savings and household expenses, but keep their own checking and savings accounts. Each month after the couple pays their bills, each of them is reimbursed for any joint debts. Even if the husband is the only breadwinner in the house, his wife should never have to "ask" for money. They should pay the bills together so that she has a good idea of their overall debt as well as income and isn't treated as a child, kept in the dark and not bothered by overly complicated stuff like bank balances. Giving control of the money to one person in the relationship gives too much power to that person, creating an unstable situation that sets up further trouble.

Sex, on the other hand, is the first weapon used in the battle of the sexes, usually to make a point. Anger can do a number on the libido, so one of the partners withholds sex initially because she or he is really not in the mood. It's also a way of making your partner pay attention. Basically, one of the two feels that his or her needs are not being met, so since a marriage is a partnership, withholding sex is considered a quid pro quo. In the past, the sexual part of a relationship was minimized. Passion was the flame that burnt twice as bright and half as long, and if a relationship was based solely on sex, it wasn't expected to last. Long-term relationships needed things like good communication, respect, honesty, and trust. They still do, but the power of sex should not be underestimated. With the sexual revolution and the growing practice of premarital sex, couples are much better at it than they used to be. Today sex is delicious, not precious, and if it's withheld for too long in a relationship, its absence becomes magnified. It's one of the most intimate acts a couple can share, and when it's suspended, that's a very cruel form of rejection, creating a deep-seated resentment that can be difficult to eradicate.

Many couples worry unnecessarily about the amount of sex they may be having, but it really depends on the individual and the couple's own needs. Some people have great stamina and active libidos and admit to being in a constant state of horniness. Others claim that once a week or even a month is adequate. If a couple has built a solid foundation based on friendship, love, respect, trust, and honesty, and they have good lines of communication, the "how oftens" can be worked out, but if nothing is said and months turn into years, sex has definitely become a problem that needs to be addressed. Good sex is a sign of a solid relationship. According to marriage counselor Sig Taylor, "It's a barometer, and it's usually the last thing to go. If couples get to the point where there is no sexuality anymore, the relationship is pretty much dead."

LATINAS IN LOVE SURVEY

Q: Compared to other women, are you more or less shy when it comes to sex?

A: Sixty-four percent of the Latinas who responded said they were less shy, 28 percent said they were shyer, and 8 percent said they were in the middle.

In the bedroom, however, some Latinas may not be so bold as to question the situation. They were, and still are, taught never to question their husbands and to please them above all else. Times are changing, thankfully, and although they may not feel comfortable taking a scorecard into the bedroom, Latinas are hip to the joys of sex. Which comes first, good sex or good communication skills? Actually, a woman's self-confidence has a lot to do with both and should be developed before either can follow. In a 1999 article in *Maclean's*, Richard Dearing, director of the Marriage Therapy Program at the University of Winnipeg, confirmed that men use sex to feel good while women need to feel good before they get into bed. For a woman to feel good about sex, she has to feel good about herself. To enjoy sex, she has to be comfortable with who she is; she has to trust that this most imitate moment in a relationship is being shared with a man who can appreciate it. Confidence, friendship, trust, and communication will carry most relationships for the first five years. Sex only becomes an issue when it's denied.

What Is True Love?

IN THIS BOOK we've looked at many types of love available to Latinas—first love, obsessive love, mature love—but what about so-called "true" love? We know that broken hearts mend, but does that mean that all those unsuccessful relationships were merely dysfunctional loves and not true ones? Did the pain and heartache serve only to prepare us for the real deal? Even more perplexing is the fact that at the time, it "felt" like true love, so if it wasn't, how can we tell the real thing from a practice test? These are all very valid questions and the answer to all of them is a matter of opinion. I'd like to think that soul mates do exist, but according to one young Latina, the concept is a myth because the idea that somewhere out there, one person exists just for you is preposterous. "Besides, the chances of ever meeting that one person, that he'll happen to live in the same city that you live in, or even find his way there, are practically nil," she proclaims.

Granted, people don't always get it right on the first try, but in my experience, true love is a work in progress. It's not just made up of lightning bolts or fireworks, but also the mundane activities like grocery shopping or washing dishes. Novelists have written about it vividly, philosophers have talked about it ad nauseum, and psychologists have analyzed it inconclusively. The latter professions have certainly come up with countless suggestions for meeting people or keeping a relationship alive, but they haven't really captured true love. Novelists, however, occasionally hit the nail on the head and because they deal in fantasy, they appeal strongly to women. Novelists can create the perfect scenario and what they don't write, the reader will usually orchestrate in her own mind. Inevitably, the characters in these tomes will answer the eternal question: How do you know when you've found true love?

LOVE IN LITERATURE

These novels are among the greatest love stories ever written, and prove that there are many different and powerful kinds of love.

Pride and Prejudice—"true" love
Wuthering Heights—dysfunctional love
Gone with the Wind—manipulative love
Like Water for Chocolate—sacrificial love
Kiss of the Spider Woman—fantasy love

Romeo and Juliet, for whom Shakespeare named his tragic play, were young lovers, Heathcliff and Catherine, in Emily Brontë's brooding *Wuthering Heights*, were dysfunctional lovers, and Margaret Mitchell's Scarlet and Rhett in *Gone with the Wind* were manipulative control freaks. There are several other examples of powerful love relationships in fiction, but for me, the quintessential "true love" is the love shared by Elizabeth Bennett and Fitzwilliam Darcy in Jane Austen's classic novel *Pride and Prejudice*. Never out of print since it was first published in 1813, the book continues to strike a romantic chord in readers to this day and I think it aptly communicates the message I've tried to convey to you in these pages about self-worth and love. At a glance, the novel could be considered sappy tripe that only reinforces outmoded and repressed ideas about male and female relationships. After all, the premise of the story isn't far removed from the film *How to Marry a Millionaire*. But anyone who's made this assumption is mistaken. Despite its age, *Pride and Prejudice* still tells the tale of modern romance. The heroine, a strong, confident, intelligent young woman, is faced with the fact that she may never marry because of her social position. Eventually, she's challenged to compromise her principles and to question her own judgment in the face of both eligible and ineligible suitors.

The options for women in the early nineteenth century were few. Middle-class young women either had to marry well to improve their prospects or face a life of dependency on their nearest relatives. If the right husband didn't come along and there were few relatives on whom to depend, some of these women would pursue a career in education, either as a governess or teacher. For ladies of the English gentry, their lives involved taking long walks, sewing embroidered panels, and otherwise waiting to exhale. In Jane Austen's story, the lead character is not technically a lady of the gentry, but she is a gentleman's daughter. She has no prospects for wealth because she is the second oldest of five girls. Without brothers, the family has no immediate heirs to provide for the sisters. As was required by law, all property was entailed onto male heirs, so upon Mr. Bennet's death, his property goes to the next male heir, who happens to be a distant cousin. Clearly, Elizabeth and her sisters must marry well, but their lives are further complicated and their prospects limited by a tactless mother and two boy-crazy younger sisters who can find nothing better to do first thing in the morning than walk into town and check out the army officers.

The genius of this book is Elizabeth. She's no shrinking violet, pining away for her Prince Charming. She's smart and realistic, yet still romantic. She has honestly assessed her situation, but she's also not willing to settle when it comes to love. She knows that her good looks and sparkling wit will not be enough to raise her prospects, but she's not going to marry for any other reason but love. With this attitude, she also understands that she may end up the favorite spinster aunt of her sisters' children. The path to true love will not be simple for any of the Bennet sisters, but Elizabeth's is particularly interesting. Austen doesn't introduce just any man for Elizabeth. She chooses one of the richest and most handsome men in the county to be her suitor. Neither of the two makes a particularly strong impression on the other when they meet. For Elizabeth, although Mr. Darcy is certainly good looking, he's also extremely proud and full of himself. For Mr. Darcy, she's well below him socially and although he finds her fairly attractive, he considers her family situation extremely unappealing. After one particularly witty exchange between the two, Austen writes: "Darcy had never been so bewitched by any woman as he was by her. He really believed that were it not for the inferiority of her connections, he should be in some danger."

We know from the title that pride and prejudice will factor into the story, and Austen introduces both faults fairly quickly. Mr. Darcy, is "proud and disagreeable," while Elizabeth is sure she has him pegged correctly from the get-go and is immediately prejudiced against him when she hears the story of an injustice Mr. Darcy committed against the son of his father's steward. She hears it from the son himself, Mr. Wickham, and doesn't doubt him for a moment or even question the impropriety he exhibits by sharing such a personal and private story with her, a complete stranger. The novel continues with several opportunities for conflict. She is thrown together with Mr. Darcy socially because her mother has noticed that his wealthy and friendly best friend, Mr. Bingley, has shown an interest in her oldest daughter, Jane. Their interaction, however, does nothing to improve Elizabeth's opinion of Darcy. He, on the other hand is not so lucky. On second and third looks, Elizabeth improves tremendously, assisted also by her personality, which is playful and witty. Despite his best efforts to fight his feelings, he falls for her hard and halfway through the book, proposes. At first, Elizabeth is surprised by his proposal, but when she catches his expression, completely confident and smug, certain that his proposal will not be refused, she responds accordingly. Her decision is further supported by the fact that while he's professing his love, he's also expressing his disgust with her family and the "inferiority" of her connections. To this, she responds, "In such cases as these, it is, I believe, the established mode to express a sense of obligation for the sentiments avowed, however unequally they may be returned. It is natural that obligation should be felt, and if I could feel gratitude, I would now thank you. But I cannot—I have never desired your good opinion, and you have certainly bestowed it most unwillingly. I am sorry to have occasioned pain to anyone. It has been most unconsciously done, however, and I hope will be of short duration."

Her refusal is perfect. In the modern vernacular, it could be summed up in a snappy, "As if." But in the more eloquent manner of the Edwardians, she lets him know that even if he were the richest man in the world, she still deserves more than what he's willing to offer her. When he accuses her of refusing him because he hurt her pride with his honesty, she retorts, "You are mistaken, Mr. Darcy, if you suppose that the mode of your declaration affected me in any other way, than as it spared me the concern which I might have felt in refusing you, had you behaved in a more gentleman-like manner. You could not have made me the offer of your hand in any possible way that would have tempted me to accept it." Brava! Even though the concept didn't exist at the time, the book is all about Girl Power, and Elizabeth embodies it. She knows that considering her situation, she'll be thought a fool for refusing such a man, but she has a strong enough sense of her own self worth that she remains true to her inner voice. The book, of course, can't end there. The second half involves a transformation for them both. Desperately smitten, Mr. Darcy abandons his pride and instead, works to make Elizabeth like him. For her part, Elizabeth begins to realize that she may have been mistaken about this proud, disagreeable man. Just when they're about to admit their true feelings, fate intervenes. Elizabeth's younger sister runs off, unmarried, with Mr. Wickham, now revealed as a notorious scoundrel and the same young man who had attempted to run off with Mr. Darcy's sister. Convinced that any chance they might have had is now lost forever with this new family scandal, Elizabeth concedes that in the end, it is Mr. Darcy whom she loves. Thankfully, the author is Jane Austen and she likes happy endings. Things work out in the end and in a way that confirms for Elizabeth, as well as the reader, the Mr. Darcy is honorable and a gentleman.

What makes their love true, in my mind, is that their relationship combines passion, intelligence, and maturity. The passion is clear from Mr. Darcy's side. He's an intense character, rich, handsome, and haughty, but none of that protects him and the girl clearly gets under his skin. They're both intelligent, but Elizabeth is a fairly heroic figure for her time. I first read this book when I was about twelve years old and she inspired me. She became my hero and role model for the type of young woman I wanted to become. I loved that she stood up for herself, in such a smart way, and that she was able to bring this man to his knees over his love for her. Once she realized that she was looking at the man through a lens distorted by her own prejudice, she began to appreciate him. "She began not to comprehend that he was exactly the man, who, in disposition and talents, would most suit her. His understanding and temper, though unlike her own, would have answered all her wishes. It was an union that must have been to the advantage of both; by her ease and liveliness, his mind might have been softened, his manners improved, and from his judgment, information, and knowledge of the world, she must have received benefit of greater importance."

Finally, their love was gradual. They didn't get crushes and then try to turn that into something more. They really got to know each other, and it was knowing each other better that turned them into lovers. Elizabeth and Mr. Darcy spent time together socially, so they got to know each other on that level first. When Elizabeth reviewed her past conversations, she saw that the man was not what she first thought him to be and began to appreciate his efforts to be agreeable, his softened manner, and his torment. Mr. Darcy, on the other hand, was impressed by Elizabeth's mind and her personality, but because he initially considered himself superior to her and felt that marrying her was doing her a great favor, he had little hope that Elizabeth would ever forgive him, much less like him, but he was compelled to try and show her his better side. Elizabeth didn't make him change, but certainly knowing her made him choose to be a better man. She humbled him, but he was also a big enough person to admit his mistakes. For her part, she remained open to the truth, and when she realized her mistake she allowed herself to change her opinion of Mr. Darcy and see his real character. In the end, their love made them both better people.

People fall in love for different reasons. According to Gloria Steinem in *Revolution from Within* (1992) we tend to fall in love with people who represent the characteristics we're lacking, who make us feel whole, or rather, we "romanticize" that this is what true love is all about. She uses Brontë's characters Heathcliff and Catherine to explain "romantic" love. "The romance between Catherine and Heathcliff had been the result of an inner void within each of them, and the story tells of their impossible effort to fill it with the body and soul of the other." But true love is not dysfunctional. It can only take place when two people who are complete individuals come together. "Romance is a means to the end of self-completion, but love is an end in itself," writes Steinem. "If we love someone, we want them to continue being the essence of themselves. If so, then we can't own, absorb, or change them. We can only help them to become what they already are."

What all this means is that true love complements the good stuff that a couple brings to a relationship, which is why it stands the test of time. All relationships require work from time to time, but much of the time, true love is effortless. You don't notice it, and time flies while you're in it, until one day, it's your silver wedding anniversary and yet you feel like you've been together half as long. True love is not invulnerable and the usual factors that will put stress on a relationship—money, children, and sex—will still come up. But because true love is based on honesty, respect, and trust, couples should be able to talk their way through any crisis.

LATINAS IN LOVE SURVEY

When asked if their attitude toward relationships was traditional or modern, 47 percent chose modern, 44 percent chose traditional, and 9 percent said both.

Words of Experience

FINALLY, I THOUGHT it would be good to hear from Latinas who have dated, fallen in love, married, and divorced. Theories are fine, but women who have loved and lost have much to share. Looking over the surveys, I was struck by the wisdom they imparted. "Listen to your intuition for guidance. Know the person at least a year," advised one woman who has been married for only a year and a half. "Get to know each other and talk, talk, talk, and not just about superficial issues," wrote another who has been married for four years. "Be true to yourself, and you have to love yourself before you can love another," stated one Latina whose marriage ended after three years. "Always be prepared for the unexpected, and never allow a man to convince you that he is superior to you. A woman must always remember that she is capable of just as much as a man and probably even better at it," encouraged another who has been married for five years.

From these Latinas to all Latinas in love, that's pretty great advice.

Appendix
Latinas in Love Survey

What is your age?

    15–20 ❑   21–26 ❑   27–32 ❑   33–40 ❑

    41-50 ❑   51–60 ❑   over 60 ❑

What is your ethnicity?

    Non-Hispanic white ❑   Non-Hispanic black ❑

    Latina ❑   Native American ❑   Asian ❑   other ❑

Where were you born? (country, city, state)

Where do you live? (country, city, state)

What is your religious affiliation?

    Catholic ❑   Protestant ❑   Jew ❑   Christian ❑

    Muslim ❑   Buddhist ❑   other ❑   none ❑

How many years of formal education do you have?

    1–6 (grade school) ❑   6–12 (high school) ❑

    12–16 (bachelor's degree) ❑   16–20 (master's degree) ❑

over 20 (Ph.D.) ❑

Are you employed?

Yes ❑   No ❑

Is your job considered ...?

blue collar (manual labor) ❑

pink collar (clerical/secretarial) ❑

white collar (professional/managerial) ❑

What is your annual income?

below $10,000 ❑ $10,000–$15,000 ❑

$15,000–$20,000 ❑ $20,000–$30,000 ❑

$30,000–$40,000 ❑ $40,000–$50,000 ❑

$50,000–$100,000 ❑   above $100,000 ❑

What is your marital status?

Married ❑   Single ❑   Divorced ❑

Unmarried (living together) ❑

How many years?

Married_____   Single_____   Divorced_____

Unmarried (living together)_____

What is your parents' marital status and for how many years?

Married_____   Single_____   Divorced_____

Unmarried (living together)_____

What ethnicity is your mother?

    Non-Hispanic white ❑   Non-Hispanic black ❑

    Latino ❑   Native American ❑   Asian ❑

    other (please specify) ❑ _____

What ethnicity is your father?

    Non-Hispanic white ❑   Non-Hispanic black ❑   Latino ❑

    Native American ❑   Asian ❑   other (please specify) ❑ _____

What is your ethnic preference in a mate and why?

    Non-Hispanic white ❑   Non-Hispanic black ❑   Latino ❑

    Native American ❑   Asian ❑   other (please specify) ❑

Compared to non-Latinos, which of the following best describes Latino men?

    less modern ❑   equally modern ❑   more modern ❑

Compared to Latinos, which of the following best describes non-Latino men?

    less romantic ❑   equally romantic ❑   more romantic ❑

What is your age preference in a mate?

    much younger (more than ten years) ❑

    younger (five to ten years) ❑   same age ❑

    older (five to ten) ❑   much older (more than ten years) ❑

Do you support the women's movement?

 not at all ❑   somewhat ❑   absolutely ❑

Has the women's movement included women of color?

Compared to other women, are you more or less timid when it comes to sex?

 less ❑   more ❑

Which best describes your attitude toward relationships?

 modern ❑   traditional ❑

At what age did you lose your virginity? (optional)

At what age should a woman lose her virginity? Please mark the following ages with an X for too young, a Y for just right, and a Z for too old.

12–13 _____	22–24 _____
14–15 _____	25–30 _____
16–17 _____	31–35 _____
18-19 _____	35–40 _____
20-21 _____	over 40 _____

At what age should a man lose his virginity? Please mark the following ages with an X for too young, a Y for just right, and a Z for too old.

12–13_____	22–24_____
14–15_____	25–30_____
16–17_____	31–35_____
18–19_____	35–40_____
20–21_____	over 40_____

How many lovers should a woman have before getting married?
None ❑   a few (five or less) ❑   some (ten or less) ❑
a lot (20 or less) ❑   as many as possible ❑   no opinion ❑

How many lovers should a man have before getting married?
None ❑   a few (five or less) ❑   some (ten or less) ❑
a lot (20 or less) ❑   as many as possible ❑   no opinion ❑

What's the best advice your mother ever gave you about dating?

What's the worst advice your mother ever gave you about dating?

What is the best advice your mother ever gave you about marriage?

What is the worst advice your mother ever gave you about marriage?

Please rank the following components of a marriage in order of importance:

communication_____   equality_____   tenderness_____

money_____   sex_____   romance_____

children_____   honesty_____   excitement_____

love_____   humor_____   compatibility_____

Do you have brothers?

If so, are they older or younger?

Should women assume that all men are ...?
    Dogs ❏   Human beings ❏   they shouldn't assume ❏

Is it possible to have sex with a man and not fall in love?

What does it mean when a man has sex with a woman but tells her he just wants to be friends?
    that he's not ready for a relationship at this time, but may be ready later ❏
    that he just wants to be friends ❏
    that he's really in love but doesn't know it ❏

Do you believe that having sex on the first date is a good idea?
    always ❏   usually ❏   sometimes ❏   never ❏

Can you get a man to fall in love by having sex with him?

Can you get a man to marry you by living with him?

What is your idea of the perfect date?

What is your idea of a bad date?

What do you think is your best asset?

What do you think men consider your best asset?

What is your worst fault?

What do you think men consider your worst fault?

QUESTIONS FOR SINGLES
(NEVER BEEN MARRIED)

How often do you go on dates?

Would you consider meeting someone through the Internet?

What traits are you looking for in a mate?

Are you involved in a steady relationship? If yes, for how long?

What do you love most about your boyfriend?

Would you like to marry him?

QUESTIONS FOR MARRIED WOMEN

How long have you been married?

How did you meet your husband?

What most attracted you to your husband?

How long did you date?

Did you live together before you got married? If so, for how long?

How much experience did you have before getting married? (optional)
none ❏   very little ❏   some ❏   a lot ❏   tons ❏

How much experience did your husband have?
none ❏   very little ❏   some ❏   a lot ❏   tons ❏

Is your sex life?
     active ❏   somewhat active ❏   cooling off ❏
     practically nonexistent ❏

What is your husband's ethnicity?

Latino ❑   Non-Hispanic white ❑

Non-Hispanic black ❑   other ❑

If your husband is Latino, what are the advantages and disadvantages of marrying a Latino?

If your husband is non-Latino, what are the advantages and disadvantages of marrying a non-Latino?

Is your husband a mamma's boy?

Does your husband expect you to assume the traditional duties of a wife?

Does your husband consider the marriage more of a partnership, sharing equally in household as well as financial responsibilities?

Do you have children and if so, how many?

How would you like to see the marriage improved?

What is the most romantic thing your husband has ever done?

QUESTIONS FOR DIVORCÉES

How long were you married?

What attracted you to your husband(s)?

What would you look for today in an ideal mate?

Are you interested in remarrying?

Have you remarried? If so, how many times?

Did you and your ex-husband utilize a marriage counselor?

What have you learned from your failed marriage(s)?

Could the marriage have been saved; if so, how?

What advice would you give to anyone about to get married?

THE END

Thanks again. Please feel free to add comments, feedback about the survey, or any additional information.

Acknowledgments

$\mathscr{T}$HIS IS MY second book for Marlowe & Company, which affords me another opportunity to thank my publisher Matthew Lore and my editor Sue McCloskey, as well as my agent Laura Dail, for their continued support of my work. For her expertise, thanks also to Melanie Cole, my friend and mentor, who provided additional editing on the book.

Particular thank yous for this book, however, go to all the lovely ladies who took the time to respond to the Latinas in Love survey. Without their help, Latinas in Love would lack some of its most poignant moments; the opinions and thoughts imparted by these women. To my sister Lisa who offered her expert opinion and assistance in constructing and distributing the survey and to the many friends who made an extra effort to get the survey into the hands of more women, I am especially grateful. *Muchisimas gracias:* Ana Radelat, Christine Granados, Elva Guerra, Julie Chapa, Laura Dail, Nancy De los Santos, and the super *comadre,* Nora Comstock. To all the members of Las Comadres of Austin, Texas, *estoy super agradecida.*

To those who sent letters to Pilar at *Moderna* so many years ago and to the Amiga Mía readers at Hispanic Online (www.hispaniconline. com), *gracias* and keep those letters coming.

Finally, to my family, whose constant faith and encouragement makes everything I do possible. In keeping with the theme of this book, a special thanks to the three significant Menard women in my life—my sister Julie who was my partner and confidant growing up, my sister Lisa who was our role model and advisor, and my little *mamita,* Elisa, who always said the right thing.